T0372184

Drowning in Wheat

JOHN KINSELLA is the author of over forty books.
He is a Fellow of Churchill College, Cambridge University, and
Professor of Literature and Sustainability at Curtin University.
In 2007 he received the Fellowship of Australian Writers
Christopher Brennan Award for lifetime achievement in poetry,
and in 2013 was awarded the Australian Prime Minister's
Literary Award for Poetry.

Also by John Kinsella in Picador

Sack

Armour

Shades of the Sublime & Beautiful

John Kinsella

Drowning in Wheat

Selected Poems 1980–2015

PICADOR

First published 2016 by Picador
an imprint of Pan Macmillan
20 New Wharf Road, London N 1 9RR
Associated companies throughout the world
www.panmacmillan.com

ISBN 978-1-4472-2148-7

Copyright © John Kinsella 2016

The right of John Kinsella to be identified as the
author of this work has been asserted by him in accordance
with the Copyright, Designs and Patents Act 1988.

'VI', 'XXXI', 'XXXIV', 'LV': the first two lines of each of these sonnets is taken from the
Love Sonnets of Zora Cross (from *Songs of Love and Life*, Angus & Robertson Ltd., Sydney, 1917).
'Envoy', 'Goat', 'Hair', 'Kangaroos in the Fog', 'Mea Culpa', 'Red Shed', 'Reptile Life', 'Sacred Kingfisher',
from *Jam Tree Gully: Poems* by John Kinsella, copyright © 2012 by John Kinsella.
Used by permission of W.W. Norton & Company. Inc.

All rights reserved. No part of this publication may be reproduced,
stored in a retrieval system, or transmitted, in any form, or by any means
(electronic, mechanical, photocopying, recording or otherwise)
without the prior written permission of the publisher.

1 3 5 7 9 8 6 4 2

A CIP catalogue record for this book is available from the British Library.

This book is sold subject to the condition that it shall not, by way of
trade or otherwise, be lent, hired out, or otherwise circulated without
the publisher's prior consent in any form of binding or cover other than
that in which it is published and without a similar condition including
this condition being imposed on the subsequent purchaser.

Visit **www.picador.com** to read more about all our books
and to buy them. You will also find features, author interviews and
news of any author events, and you can sign up for e-newsletters
so that you're always first to hear about our new releases.

For Tracy Ryan and George Steiner

Contents

Notes on Fire-tumbles

i

Fire-tumbles roll inward
from a desert's edge.

At first they appear as
cart-wheeling spinifex,

later, flame beyond sight
takes hold, enthralled.

ii

It has been said
their substance is
of lost forest —

breath of dried air
unable to take hold.

Consumed, moved in wind.
Sand.

iii

Back through shadow
they stretch sunset
to unimaginable limits:

enveloped sky,
cinnabar of abyss.

iv

Eyes harden and fall.
Fire-tumbles, seen in
vision, last an instant.

In desert the light
of fission lingers.

v

Fire-tumbles are not poetry,
nor even a substitute for poetry.

They are things wild
whose wanderings
are without motive.

Finches

SALT PADDOCKS

Down below the dam
there is nothing but salt,
a slow encroachment.

Fighting back, my cousins
have surrounded it
with a ring of trees.

At its centre
lives a colony of finches,
buried in tamarisks.

FINCH COLONY

The leaves, like wire, are so tangled
we dare not venture too far into their heart
where flashes of song and dull colour
betray a whole family of finches.

We hold our breath
and become statues.

Is this fear of disturbing their peace
or of a delicate raid from unknown spaces.

[3]

FINCH FLIGHT

To join the finch
in his tenuous kingdom
amongst tamarisks,
the hot snow of salt

You must gather
trajectory and direction,
sharp summer flights

Exile yourself
from the wind's hand.

FINCH DEATH

The dead finch lies on salt,
tight-winged and stretched.

The others shimmer
loosely in heat

the salt's white mystery
coveting tin cans, skull of sheep.

Slowly, death rides this hot glacier
further and further away.

[4]

Links

'Every separation is a link . . .'
— Simone Weil

i.

There are days when the world
buckles under the sun, trees blacken
to thin wisps, spinifex fires,
and white cockatoos, strangled
in telegraph wire, hang
dry and upside down.

ii.

I think only of thirst.
The drifting sand does not
lend itself to description,
the sketchy border trees
offer little protection
from the sun as we negotiate
the edge and fine line
between sand and vegetation.

iii.

I have always lived by the sea,
or travelling underground, have always
been concerned with water — the flooding
of mines, rain in dark forests,
the level of the tide.

iv.

To see a waterbird, maybe a crane,
fly deep into desert, comes as no
surprise — we note its arrival and follow
its disappearance, discuss it over a beer,
and think nothing more of it.

v.

And nights, contracting into cool winds,
when the sand becomes an astrolabe to the stars,
where in the reflection of the crystal spheres
we wander without direction, searching out
water flowers . . .

Night Parrots

If at all, then fringe dwellers
　　　　of the centre.
Ghosts of samphire, navigators
of the star-clustered tussocks.
Of salty marsh, limestone niches,
　　　　and acrid airs.

If at all, then flitting obscurely
the rims of water tanks, the outlands
of spotlights and filaments of powerlines . . .
in brief nocturnal flight, with *long
drawn-out mournful whistle.*

If at all, then moths in a paper lantern.

Fire-eaters at Lasseter's Reef

A troupe of fire-eaters
stumbled on Lasseter's Reef

For seven days and nights
they entertained

throwing vast jets of flame
out over desert

Having seen
their repertoire

he grew bored and desired
conversation

but their every breath
produced nothing but gold.

Sick Woman

Don't. Crow and butcher bird
    over garden
    over sand
    over me and sick woman.
Don't.
    Of sick woman, butcher bird
brings crow to ground, crow or
butcher bird fall, brought to ground
by sick woman. What is it we feel?
A draught, maybe as we catch
the falling crow or butcher bird
by sash of light, sash of window
Sick woman, and me told I look
like a little yellow Valium pill,
rising to the scuffling crow,
butcher bird, sick woman.

The Black Sun

As the morning rises out of the city's
Trailing archipelago and over the first trains
Breaking ice on their cold steel tracks,
We shall walk down past the blackbird trees,
The shadows of buildings close pressed,
The dull eyes of the Unknowing.
And as you head North, I'll leave
The station, follow your rumour
Through the dark clockwork of winter,
Damp market place, squalid streets,
Acacias by the harbour. And like
An ambassador called home at time of war,
Step onto an Eastern ferry, always knowing
That a black sun hung over our parting.

Inland

Inland: storm tides,
ghosts of a sheep weather
alert, the roads uncertain

families cutting the outback
gravel on Sunday mornings,
the old man plying the same track
to and from the session
those afternoons, evenings
(McHenry skidded into a thickset
mallee after a few too many
and was forced to sell up)

On the cusp of summer
an uncertain breeze
rises in grey wisps
over the stubble —
the days are ashen,
moods susceptible,
though it does not take
long to get back
into the swing of things

We take the only highroad
for miles as the centre
of the primum mobile — it's
the eye of the needle

through which our lives'
itineraries must be drawn,
a kind of stone theodolite
measuring our depths beyond
the straight and narrow,
it's a place of borrowed dreams
where the marks of the spirit
have been erased by dust —
the restless topsoil

Old Hands/New Tricks

A ring-necked parrot drops into flight,
fence posts collapse and ossify,
the wattle bird trims the lamp of wattle bloom

Despite storm weather the soaks diminish,
though by way of contrast the green tinge
of a late rain pokes its head over stubble —
the new growth that will yield no seed

About the homestead unripe fruit is severed
from trees — parrots jostle, making
swings and see-saws of their bodies

The wells are covered with railway sleepers
over-run with wire-weed and Mediterranean
Bugloss — Salvation Jane — which crisps over
cracks, gives cool water a taste of irony

In the pepper trees magpies threaten to unpick
the world as they know it — their songs are not
characteristic — old hands have learnt new tricks

Two Days Before Harvest

An easterly stretches and compresses
deadwood fissures, strings of parakeets
arrange themselves into nets to drag
the breeze — their feathers firing,
sun striking the afternoon pink.

In the soon-to-be-lopped heads of wheat
there burns the fidelity of summer — beyond,
on the white-bake of salt, lines of supply
are thinning and the dust of scuffed patches
drinks the blood of eucalypts. Topknot pigeons
encounter themselves, much to their surprise,
in foray from she-oak to powerline and back again.

The tines of a discarded scarifier have set
like roots of trees ringbarked from memory —
you see, the tractor's welter, the jiggering
blades of the header, the crows teasing
gate-posts, unlock a continuity
that would persist, or threaten to . . .

The Myth of the Grave

i

A pair of painted quails
scurries across the quills of stubble
a flurry of rapid
eye movement

they shadow my walk
ostentatiously
lifting and dropping
into invisible alleyways

reaching the grave
I turn to catch them
curving back, stopped
by the windrows

the grave is a magnet
that switches polarity
when you reach it.

ii

The epitaph is measured
by the size of the plaque,
or is it the plaque that's
measured by the epitaph?

It seems to matter.
Death becomes a question
of economy — the lavish are big
on ceremony, slight on prayer.

iii

At a distance
sheep leave salt-licks
beside a dam and zig-zag
down towards the shade.

Grey gums bend with the tide
of the breeze, the midday sun
would carry their doubles
to the grave and fill the urns.

The ground dries and crumbles,
a lizard darts out of a crack
and races across the paddock.
Do ashes rest easily here?

iv

A fresh grave that holds three
generations is something you question
on a first encounter. How in life
would they have felt about sharing

a single room in a shoebox flat?
Maybe, at an instant, only one soul
is resident, the others entering the bodies
of quails, exploring the wastes of stubble.

Pillars of Salt

We always look back,
attracted by that feeling
of having been there before — the roads
sinking, the soil weeping (scab on scab
lifted), fences sunk to gullies
catching the garbage of paddocks,
strainers blocked by stubble
and machinery and the rungs
of collapsed rainwater tanks / and maybe
the chimney and fireplace
of a corroded farmhouse, once
the guts of the storm, now
a salty trinket.

The salt is a frozen waste
in a place too hot for its own good,
it is the burnt-out core of earth's eye,
the excess of white blood cells.
The ball-and-chain rides lushly
over its polishing surface, even dead wood
whittles itself out of the picture.

Salt crunches like sugar-glass, the sheets
lifting on the soles of shoes (thongs scatter
pieces beyond the hope of repair) — finches
and flies quibble on the thick fingers
of salt bushes, a dugite spits
blood into the brine.

An airforce trainer jet appears,
the mantis pilot — dark eyed and wire
jawed — sets sight on the white wastes
for a strafing run: diving, pulling out
abruptly, refusing to consummate.
                                        Salt
explodes silently, with the animation
of an inorganic life, a sheep's skull no more
than its signature, refugees already
climbing towards the sun
on pillars of salt.

Catchment

i zone

In a catchment zone the keepers
must keep clean houses, sweeping
soot from the roots, scouring
granite outcrops regularly.

The catchment's focus — a saline pool,
comfortable in its illusion of deep, clear water —
sheds itself in the stubs of severed trees
hedging the waterline.

ii quarry

Examining the dross of a quarry
(the coarse and fine sizes), we may grasp
what it is that has reduced things to this:

the panorama sliced away in cross section,
exposing the roots in their bed of rock;
or in the deeper layers, the mechanism driving
the rust of ironface, feeding the surface's scrub,
slipped buttresses, cliff faces . . .

                                  the risk of overextension
threatening the pristine catchment:
the quarry top seeking to cover the wounds.

iii   pipes and valves

We scale the wall, rising up over the filaments
of pumping station — pipes, straitjacketed,
annelids splitting and regenerating in and out
of the slinking earth, skirting the valley,
entwining undergrowth

                        the valves feeding
from their concrete outriggers (weir-houses
inhabited by pressure gauges, clacks, and screws),
their task reason enough for existence, thoughts
on source and destination not one of their strong points.

iv   the wider waters

Sloughs of mosquitoes squeezing in and out
of sluices in a hillside cast barely
a collective shadow over the catchment.

At the foot of a spillway, past seasons
wallow in brackish puddles, raft insects
eke out sketchy existences
                        thin lines of pines
cling to retainer walls.

From the summit — the barrier neither moulded nor bound
by roots, but soldered to the squared shoulders
of valley — we look to the liquid centre: wind slicks
flattening the ripples, ironing them out, wiping
the corrugated glass clean, darning patches
on the wider waters.

The Orchardist

Orange trees cling
to the tin walls
of his home. A red
checked shirt and grey
pair of trousers hang
over the one-eyed tractor.
His oranges are small suns
and he is an astronaut
floating slowly
through their spheres.
of influence.

Black Suns

The orchard, canker-bound and fading — Australian
Gothic. A bladeless windmill remonstrates

with a warm wind as it singes
oranges scattered in bitter wreaths

of deadwood, scale, and vitrified leaves.
A black-winged kite wrestles with temptation

and logic — water rats scaling the ruins
of barbed wire fences. The season equivocates.

I remove my shoes, the water stretches
bulrushes like new strings on an old guitar.

I position the wreck of my body and wait.
There is arrogance in this — expecting

him to appear, to consider his withering fruit,
divine my return, while refusing to cross

and help drag black suns from their sick zodiacs
with the hook of his walking stick.

A Field of White Butterflies

There is a lot of mystery in me . . .
he explains, peering deep into my eyes.
*As a child I would examine the smallest
things, things that would not ordinarily
be seen. My mother would tell the neighbours
that I was a daydreamer, there was no other way
of explaining it. That was in a very
cold place, high in the mountains
above Dalmatia in Yugoslavia.
I came here when I was eighteen
looking for work. I knew about
the languages of animals and plants.*

*Three seasons ago you couldn't
look at this paddock without seeing
a white butterfly — consuming, crowding
even themselves out of existence.
Last season I saw two, two white butterflies
in the whole year. This year the Monarch
will come, mark my words — wandering
down over the hills, settling
pince-nez on the potato flowers.
You see, where people settle
imbalance follows, the air
being full of white butterflies,
or there being no white butterflies at all.*

Paperbarks

Paperbarks scream out of childhood
deep into wetlands — lightning, a silver flash
of the fringe, though as subliminal as ghosts,
their territory that of the spirit.
Water fallen, dank goitres tease
our thirst, skins peel and flake
about the grasping roots, sweltering
in the red tinge of earth. Though holding light
absorbent skins will not extinguish when voice
falls and memory lingers, for these are ghosts
who sing the stagnant weathers,
and brew storms out of drought.

The Bottlebrush Flowers

A Council-approved replacement
for box trees along the verges
of suburban roads, it embarrasses
with its too sudden blush — stunning
at first, then a burning reminder
of something you'd rather forget.
And it unclothes so ungraciously —
its semi-clad, mangy, slovenly,
first-thing-in-the-morning appearance.
And while I've heard it called
a bristling firelick, a spiral
of Southern Lights, I've also seen
honey-eaters bob upside down
and unpick its light in seconds.

Plumburst

for Wendy

The neat greens of Monument Hill
roll into sea, over the rise the soft rain
of plumfall deceives us in its groundburst.

If lightning strikes from the ground up,
and Heaven is but an irritation that prompts
its angry spark, then plums are born
dishevelled on the ground and rise
towards perfection . . .

Out of the range of rising plums
we mark the territory of the garden,
testing caprock with Judas trees,
pacing out melon runs. Behind us a block
of flats hums into dusk and the sun
bursts a plum mid-flight.

.

The Phenomena that Surround
A Sighting of Eclipse Island

1   The Gap: A Paradox

I speak to you elementally
and at a distance
that becomes
the depth
of an ocean
that in being southern
and arctic
in impression
absorbs all blues
and is the deeper for this.

Darkness wells
from the fathoms
of the palette
as I paint
an expression —
my footholds
prone to slippage:
hard rock stacked
like soft lozenges
sucked by cyclopean
giants who'd smashed
aside savage breakers
to sear bone-black cliffs —

like The Gap
through which I peer; place
of the freak wave,
back-stabbing gale,
and brutal rain.

Place where
a neighbour
of my brother's
threw herself
mandraxed and furious
into this suicide
machine only
to survive
and find herself
a landlubber
farming children
with the names
of sea-nymphs. Place
where keening landfall
sea-meets and rifles
moods, like a gale
springing the bleak staves
of a broken container ship.
Place where phenomena
shape themselves like
the vertebrae of whales
tormented by water,
wind, and sun —
anchored to the coastline

by harpoons requisitioned
from the magazines
of scuttled whale-chasers
limping sulkily
icewards.

2   *The Blowholes — A Lust Recalled*

Not firing today.
Unless I've plunged
over the cliffs and into
the Prussian blue waters
without their noticing —
drawn by the spell
of Eclipse Island.
Somewhere she holds
her heart in her mouth,
clenched firmly
between pearled teeth,
his tongue flickering
about the blockage
like an astringent.

3   *Stray Pockets Of Diffident Weather*

The way rocks
just below the surface
incite the ocean,
frustrate it into action:

[31]

the flurry of white-water
luminescent greens
and the slick white
of glossy house-paint.

Consider again your foothold —
Eclipse Island spiriting
the sheets of solidified flesh,
the stray pockets
of diffident weather
moving between fronts.

4   *Eclipse Island?*

Well, I was just waiting
and then I got to thinking
about lighthouses — I could see
two of them from my *vantage point* — one
on the mainland, another on Eclipse Island;
and I thought of the candy-striped
lighthouse I'd shown you in Geraldton
and of that lighthouse just down
from your sister's place looking like
a white bishop from our chess set.
And I realised how easy it would be
for others to misconstrue my missing you
(as). Anyway, it's just not true.

5   *The Ship's Log: The Colophon*

Sheer
waste
this spray
moving skywards
like
an inverted
parachute.
The sun drinks
in the layers
holding
heavy weather
close
to the water.
We shape
an itinerary
of arrivals
and departures.
A footnote
is added
like bad breath
to a deep kiss
in an impressionable
place —
later in life
they dressed well
and cared
generally
about

their
appearance.
The ship's log full
I make
for shore.

6   *The Camera*

Why do you give me
so many opportunities to make a fool
of you anyway? You ask?
Like the tourist
caught on the lip of The Gap
unable to edge his way back,
the camera about his neck
tapping at the rocks
like a sick pendulum,
his head weighing
more than it should.

7   *Ultramarine: The Puzzle Solved*

Breath, an icy pocket,
opens ultramarine,
a dry sea
tracking its glacial
course   beyond
Eclipse Island

and beyond
the course,
cancelling
as the tides
rip back and forth
covering all earth,
a mosaic impressed
upon the potential
arrangements
of itself.
Lapis lazuli,
a gift ultramarine,
blended in the swirl
of the sun indeterminate
above the clouds —
the locals saying
*it's just an ordinary
summer's day,*
which is their way
and our solution.

Swarm

Black fire with an orange heart
rages amongst the red branches
of the swarm-tree. I tell her it's
temporary, like last year.
The hive, high in a hollow
in the neighbours' yard, erupts
and sparks. Our son bursts
through the flywire door
screaming *bees*! as if their
frantic clamour were drums of war.
It hangs bristling and fluid,
its mystery an optical illusion.
A midday astronomy — the eye
of the telescope scorched
and holding the cold heat
of space. Towards evening
the swarm lifts and rolls
chaotically downwind,
settling its orange cowl
about the dark outline
of a tree.

Of

Of emulsifiers and preservatives
extracted from boiled-down animal,
of houses with walls of horse hair
and thongs of leather to restrain
the tortured awning,
of feet covered in dead cow,
kangaroo, crocodile . . .
the business of pig-skin briefcases,
of those whose guilt lay in fish,
of those sucking the nectars
of sacred beasts,
of the differences between *clean* and *dirty* flesh,
of those who seek truth in the burnt offering,
of 'perfect and upright' Job, slaughterer
who sought to appease over and over,
of *Julius Civilis With A Dead Cock*
arrogantly accepting what *is*
over and over, back and forth, to and fro.

Sexual Politics In Eadweard Muybridge's
Man Walking, After Traumatism Of The Head

1

He could easily be
A man walking, after traumatism
Of the head.
There's something vaguely Platonic about this.
Francis Bacon, lip-synching
His way through smugness, injecting passion and/or lust
Into Muybridge's studies of wrestlers: 'Actually,
Michelangelo and Muybridge
Are mixed up in my
Mind together, and so I perhaps
Could learn about positions
From Muybridge
And learn about the ampleness,
The grandeur of form
From Michelangelo . . .' This is not tongue-in-cheek,
And why should it be? she cries.
At the end of the day
Folly counts for nothing, she says
Majestically, the banana light glowing
Sedately by the bedhead, Foucault
Powerless and fading.

2

What moral autonomy remains
As, from frame to frame,
He walks. Why aren't you a panel beater?
She asks as your last thought spills
To the floor and scatters.

Muybridge considered
Leland Stanford's Quest To Prove
All Four Legs Of A Trotting Horse
Are Off The Ground Simultaneously
At A Particular Moment . . . earlier
He'd been a fly on the wall
As Muybridge blew his wife's
Dashing, cavalier lover away . . .
'omne animal triste post coitum'.

Sadness comes quickly
And he wonders about
The contents of his blood.
And panel beaters would find
The passive role
Difficult
To shape.

3

Sharing a cell with lust
In the prison of desire
He remarked that the form
Of his cell-mate was a little peculiar:
Casanova moving with the gait
Of one who has succumbed
To animal locomotion, an electro-photographic
Investigation of consecutive phases
Of animal movement.

She says that he measures progress
With his penis, a well-oiled dip stick:
Her body absorbing the entire jungle
Of his body which is ecologically sound,
Creeping out of its rich enclave
And seeking to make the barren lush.
He believes that you can't get off
On rape, that violence is mental
Sickness.
I like his manners — c'est tout —
She confesses.

4

A skull fractured
Does not necessarily
Mean liberation
On the afterdeath plane
Nor freedom for the oppressed mind.
LSD, a freak in drag,
Denies the mind is lodged
In the skull, that it is
Part of the body. The dozens or so
Blotters found in his pocket
Have nothing to do
With his portfolio
Of deviance.
He's on top of it,
And knows the yellow haze
Suppressing the landscape
Is merely ash
In the upper atmosphere.
The signature is this: it hurts
To cum on bad acid, but did that
ever deter you?

5

His head is traumatised
By dehydration, his brain shrinking.
Starvation has frayed the linkages
Between spinal cortex and legs.
His walk is one of decline
Interrupted by hope.
He feels spent and thin.
Men eat to vomit and vomit to eat,
Seneca tells us; and no woman can be too rich or too thin.
Chastity is starvation
Starvation is traumatism of the head.

6

She hates the hype
But loves the splendour:
The page written she relinquishes
Her rights to the material
Inherently hers. The moral community
Is concerned only with growth
At the end of the day — he tells them
That he is hers and couldn't give a shit.
Does she reciprocate? they say.
Would you — a man walking,
With a traumatism of the head?

7

Underwire bras and jockstraps
Entangle a chicken desperately
Lunging, a torpedo already
Within range of its tail feathers,
Rudely muzzling its way
Through a sea of discharge.
So, this is love? it asks.
Muybridge screams from his observation post
'Keep the bloody thing within the gridwork!
Calibrate, calibrate! for God's sake
It's all comparative.' Stripping off
He rushes the chicken and wrestles it,
'Damn the torpedoes, keep the cameras rolling!'
Duchamp's Nude descends a staircase
While Meissonier, de Neuville, Detaille,
Remington, Malevich, and Giacomo Balla
Watch on excitedly.

8

When size doesn't matter
You'd better start asking questions.
I mean, it's all or nothing
Isn't it. As for what's behind it . . .
A magnet *does* have *two* poles.
Self-control, the object of pleasure:
Every orgasm a spot in time
Without the lacework.
And this all about walking,
With a traumatism of the head,
The lexicon spread as three rednecks
Smash you over the skull with iron-knuckled
Fists, or an overdose of speed threatens
To burst capillaries, or glass lodged in a crescent
Below your left eye dislodges and unplugs
The contents of your identity.
The time lapse between frames shortens
And your collapse is traced
more minutely. Hasten slowly.

9

Porn is the Theory.
Rape is the Practice.
A sign held by a youth
In Minneapolis.
A skirt stained with sweat
Radiates in a bath
Of yellow dye.
The gate is locked,
The fences high.
She, sunbaking,
Looks over her shoulder,
Her tan slipping away:
In a tree perches
Her neighbour,
A glint in his eye.

10

Stripping thought
He dreamt an anthology,
Visual and responsive.
Reflections on the obvious.
A spring day and I'm full of hate.
Stuff like that.
He would include
A photograph by Muybridge
(Who after disposing of Major Larkyns
Apologised to the ladies
And settled to a newspaper).
Though not one of his locomotion
Sequences, whose implication
Goes beyond a book, but of the *Colorado*
In dry dock accompanied by an anonymous
Muybridge on Contemplation Rock
Later used as proof of madness.
And on the title page a quote
From *The San Francisco Daily*
Evening Post: 'Little
Did Muybridge dream
As he bent over
The bedside of his wife
And he caressed her,
That Larkyns' kisses
Were yet fresh and hot
Upon her lips.'

[46]

Warhols

ON ANDY WARHOL'S *Baseball*
AND *Gold Marilyn Monroe*

Marilyn a gold shrouded satellite
orbiting the American Dream, course

marked *collision*: the industrial might
of the nation pre-packed and Fort Knox poised

to catch the shrapnel should the hitters slip.
Re-runs of greatness start to look the same,

but you Marilyn retain your aura:
from the earthly DiMaggio, loaded

and ready to leap from the black bunker,
to your heavenly lips, icons worshipped

by every team, loved even in defeat.
And the celebrity pitching the first

ball of the season calls the atmosphere
sweet. The President licks your golden feet.

ON ANDY WARHOL'S *Marilyn Six-Pack*

Rip-top lips — the movement is piracy.
An early cut — an addict's selective

disclosure. A perfect pose concealing
popular truths, the value of trashy

synthetic polymer makeup, canvas
skin and silkscreened hair. A six-pack's hazy

suppression of class and style, like seeing
the world in black and white. Quick! Look at me!

it pleads with a fizzing hiss. If you stand
long enough success will expose itself.

The pout shapes the plates, but the eyelids take
the weight — suspended languidly below

the constructed eyebrows. O Marilyn —
six tabs without the blister packaging.

On Andy Warhol's *Optical Car Crash*

Movement behind the scene: no rescue can be
a complete success if there's no heartbeat

to be felt, if desolation of metal and flesh
are the motivating factor behind the picture,

if police care only that it might bring sense
to those hitting the gas pedal after a dozen

martinis at the office party. But here, motion
is heartbeat, though irregular and obviously

exposed to death (short polymer green, highly
sugared long-dried-blood red) in the painted

cardiograph. No Marilyn here. But it's nothing
to do with squeamishness or bad publicity. As

Andy realised, she'd a lot to do elsewhere.

ON WARHOL'S *Marilyn Monroe's Lips*
AND *Red Disaster*

Curse the attractiveness of the cheery
and stereotyped lushness of her lips —

the glam trap — eager — strapped tight to the moist
rollercoaster, a twitch like electric

fleas, a pout that has you bursting with a
shout outwardly bright, well fed; the spirit

just what it should be, and fluorescent teeth —
fit for an advertisement — capture and

isolate the *feminine*, like a flash
billboard — you've got to press a kiss on hers.

Red kills overkill. Expect it. Not just
pink around the gills but ripe on the love

spot. And the doctrine forms the shadow — dark
the lining of her lips, the empty chair.

A 1963 *Lavender Disaster* AND ANDY WARHOL

> 'The satellites were peaches
> waiting to be bruised.'
>   – Nat Finkelstein

The body a peach with its lavender
aura, the executioner synthetic

and imported duty free. The stage-craft
altar industrial and formatted.

Lavender disaster sucked dry dry dry
by the cold room and frame of an electric

chair — witnesses to a disaster pan
frame by frame the knee-jerk reaction, jolts

of pop conscience amongst the share-holders
of destruction: the vinyl balloons filling

the rooms of the Factory. The victims
— chic society claims — will play minor

parts anyway — mere satellites to the
colortones, a lavender celebrity.

ON WARHOL'S *Tunafish Disaster* And *Red Elvis*

Did a leak kill Mrs Brown? Did a leak
kill Mrs McCarthy? Did Elvis chill

out when faced with their cool bodies, eyelids
drooping, while he, with blurred vision could see

with thirty-six sets of eyes, still lusting
after the days when lithium was a

tasty table salt? Or when Dick Nixon
relied on him to set the kids straight and

the FBI struck a deal to make all
pink Cadillacs bleed like tuna: trusted

icons of supermarkets, suspended
in seas of air-conditioning? Elvis

gently sings the victims in their long sleep,
his red hair as slick as publicity.

On Warhol's *Blue Electric Chair*
And *Statue of Liberty*

Low energy? Uh? Partial exposure
to liberty. Andy inside the grand

ol' lady, a Frenchy: like Citroën — be
free and prosper, the market looks after

its own. Nat might take a photo later.
Some years later. Low energy makes for

maximum output — pop equation. Could
be the column of a nuclear ex-

plosion. Rise up like blue washed flame from the
chair. Souvenirs: water on the floor con-

ducting feet towards heaven. Maybe they
bury the victims of pop upside down?

Or blow the whistle on those who throw the
switch. Here, liberty lights the fuse and lives.

The Humble Gents Social Club/
Mustard Race Riot

'The thing is that, Andy growing up where he grew up, you would have expected him to feel more at ease with the poor kids. Thinking of the hours and hours he would spend talking to all the University-kids that came to interview him . . . with the egg-heads it was FEEL ME, TOUCH ME, with the slumkids it was YOU'RE BLACK, STAY BACK!'

– Nat Finkelstein

Looks like they've got a collective skin
disorder — a problem with pigment. Blank

television screens absorbing all shades,
obliterating technicolor — the

director dragging a lazy stare from
his rubbish bin vantage point. The slumkids

growing bored — art in the making. Move fast
as a mustard Alsatian bites the hand

that doesn't feed it and mustard police
grow confused — Hey! You're supposed to be black

son! Cut them! Check the colour of their blood.
Blah blah blah. But protect yourselves — never

know what's up their dirty sleeves. Poor Andy.
Gotta get him back to the Factory.

Diamond Dust Joseph Beuys À LA ANDY WARHOL

Diamond Dust Joseph Beuys — silkscreen ink
and diamond dust on synthetic polymer paint
on canvas equivocates beneath his spiritual
hat, motivation lifting him out of darkness,
chemi-luminescent or infrared or just rich.

Skippy Rock, Augusta: Warning, the Undertow

1

Oystercatchers
scout the tight rutilic
beach, rust charting

run-off locked
cross-rock up-coast
from the bolted

lighthouse
where two oceans
surge & rip & meet.

2

Immense the deep lift
seizes in gnarls & sweeps,
straight up & built

of granite. A black
lizard rounds & snorts
the froth capillaried

up towards dry-land's
limestone, hill-side
bone marrow mapped

by water. Meta-wrought,
the lighthouse distantly
elevates & turns

the crazily
bobbing history
of freak waves

and wrecks: wrought iron
& lead paint brewing
deep in capsized

sealanes, talking shop
in thick clots of language,
bubbles thundering topwards.

3

The stab-holes
of fishing poles,
small-boy whipping

boy those gate-
crashing waves releasing
shoals of wrecked

cuttlefish bleeding sepia
like swell prising
the weed-swabbed rocks

& darkly crescented beach:
crabclaw & limpet
scuttlebut

about the rubbery
swathes of kelp.
Tenebrous lash

& filigreed canopy
of dusk-spray, under-tow
of night.

Chillies

1 THE CONSERVATIVE

Not supplicants but receptors —
wanton idols
raising red tribute, the crossover
green-orange, a query
in need of editing, ingesting the anger
and soil's biteback, the soil
drinking a market economy
red being more marketable
(a humorous colour), a conservative
hotbed wanting to cling
but conscious of the constituents'
response, hasten slowly.

2 THE MIDDLE GROUND

Or chillies without seeds.
Rarely as hot, colour
as of chrysoprase, deeply attractive,
mimicking the wrought heart
of compassion.
You don't need a glass of water
even if you'd
like to think so.

3 THE RADICAL

Green is the heat,
each chilli a piece,
sweat and a repeating stomach
something to flaunt.
You grow your own
but despite rumours
don't plant on the full moon.
Slim canisters
of motivation, slick grenades
imploding.

RESIDUE

I am addicted
to chillies.
I break a red chilli
with my fingers
and spread it
through my meal.
Another false god
bringing its pleasures.

A friend needles me
another can barely
contain her laughter.
I wipe my eyes, a seed
lodges in a tear duct.
My tears are red
and pungent.
The seeds
are the hottest
part.

The Liberating Chillies

She hates them.
I'm addicted,
grow my own
and am fascinated
by the way green turns
almost black before
the sun liberates
the red. My love
of the word 'wicked'
stems from chillies.
A bad experience
with birds' eyes
actually. Ah, little
bulls' horn rhytons,
quivers of fertility
permanently erect — the fruit
mocking the delicate flower.
But I burn
my self — the seeds
hold the sharpest power
and you must sacrifice
aesthetics for pleasure.
I burn from the inside out.

CHILLI HUNT

She says that chillies
are a form of madness —
that like a crazed dog I froth
at the thought of them.
A bizarre addiction.

Maybe. Last night the moon
full if slightly kinked,
marked a kris on the skins
of chillies bent towards
its grasp, fine metal reaching

for the loadstone. Ah that crazy
tattooist the moon. Chillies
are neither mad nor sane
if they show reverence for its
persistence. For today

I hunt without words. I feel
her watching over my shoulder,
skirts teasing the grass,
the skin on my back
erupting. I continue breaking

the stalks, collecting. Some
for immediate use, others for
drying. I know the full-blown

moon hunts in the back of her
eyes, that chillies a deeper red
than mine mark time and call her
to leave me to a minor harvest.

CHILLI CATHARSIS

It fortifies my blood
against the heat
of separation —
a placebo.
Fire against fire.
Unleash your black
lightning: anti-sex,
space condensed ultra
or even collapsed.
I take I take.
This the poet
abusing language
for the sake of stasis —
the symbol as solid
as you wish. The devil's tool,
the devil's number.
Concrete. The sculpted
chilli. Like falling
on your own sword.
The heat the heat.
Fall into my burnt body
and torch your anger,
a chilli dance
for our son — fantasia
purified. Clean
but cold. Our sweat ice
on swollen cheeks. Chillies
charred at our feet.

That in their infancy
the plants are so vulnerable
appeals to me — the leaf-eaters
and sap-suckers of the garden
will defoliate, destalk,
and wizen before the sun
has risen. But fruiting,
they are rarely bothered.
But this of course is not
so remarkable when considered
comparatively. Vulnerability
heightens savagery — the cute
lion cub et al. The other
thing that fascinates me
is their sense of fait accompli —
but there is nothing in my
family tree to suggest
an onslaught of chilli.
Neither my mother nor father
can stomach them.

ARCHETYPAL CHILLIES

Are etched deep within
the human psyche — burning
seedcases bursting and re-locating
their ornamental hue. I open my
skull to your inquisitive gaze —
look, here are my chillies,
red and foreboding, hungry
for the light. See, you've done
me a favour — chillies breed on lies
but thrive on truth. They like it
both ways. Ah, if only
you'd admit to chillies — then,
then you'd understand me. The rhetoric
would flower superbly and I'd sing.
Christ, I'd sing. And you'd hear me
no matter where you hid. Your dreams
would be coloured by my song. Of chillies
and their involvement with the growth
of our souls. Of chillies and their
need for nurturing. Of the bitterness
they harvest from rejection. For this
is their strength — they are of you and I,
they are the sun's subtle rays
grown both cold and hot, they
like it both ways.

TRANSCENDENTAL CHILLIES

The weather's changing
so chillies redden
slowly. I do not expect
them to ripen according
to my programme — though I'm
told this is my way.
But a few warm days
and you can be almost
guaranteed to find them
moving from state to state.
A green chilli flatlining
and finding the other side
tolerable. Easter Friday.
The heavy clouds are rolling in.
They predicted that a week ago.
Here, try a chilli — they're
deadly at this time of year —
the pride of the garden — corn
long since finished, the last rays
of summer spilling from over-ripe
tomatoes, lettuces shaking their
seedy arms, their heads embalmed
about thickened stalks
while chillies — majestic — daggers
awaiting the sunlight, hone
their skills in the weakening light.

THE POLICE BUSTED ME
WITH A CHILLI IN MY POCKET

It'd been through the wash — it was
in fact half-a-chilli
looking fibrous and not a little
washed out. But there was
no doubting it was a chilli,
I accepted that — no need
for laboratory tests, the eye
and honesty adequate analysis.
So, why do you do it
they asked. I dunno, just a habit
I guess. The sun dropped below
the horizon like a billiard ball.
The chilli glowed in a hand.
One of them rubbed his eyes and they
began to sting. We'll have you for assault
they said.

Wireless Hill

Not seen for decades the parrot bush
made a subtle comeback — fire
liberating seeds from their long

hibernation. A twenty-eight melds
into its birth flower, camouflaging
and buzzing and cackling out of sight:

a satellite lost in crazy telemetry,
untrackable despite an atmosphere
of communication. The sea breeze, salty

and moist and full of static, zips
about the walkways and the triptych
of lookout towers, anchorage blocks

of Wireless Hill's original aerial.
With a festive glint on their bonnets,
cars unwind the radials, stereos

pursue their fractious circuits, trilling
and hissing like valve radios. And from
the central tower I look out over

Alfred Cove, and absorb the river.
You watch the children ski down slides
in the adventure playground and scoot

their bikes about the walkways, the sticky
hum that comes with rubber on hot concrete
reminding you of our son. You look

to the base of the tower, I look out —
even further than the river. But the sun
drives us towards the shade and touching

earth we hear the silent conversations
that crackle so faintly, too faint even
for aerials to detect. Yes, our son

would wade out into that cove,
over the rusty flats, bloodworms
unravelling and inciting black silt,

while pelicans, those navigation
markers for waders and migratory birds,
disappear in the space between sandbars.

Warhol at Wheatlands

He's polite looking over the polaroids
saying gee & fantastic, though always
standing close to the warm glow

of the Wonderheat as the flames
lick the self-cleansing glass.
It's winter down here & the sudden

change has left him wanting. Fog
creeps up from the gullies & toupées
the thinly pastured soil. It doesn't

remind him of America at all. But there's
a show on television about New York so
we stare silently, maybe he's asleep

behind his dark glasses? Wish Tom
& Nicole were here. He likes the laser
prints of Venice cluttering the hallway,

the sun a luminous patch trying
to break through the dank cotton air
& the security film on the windows.

Deadlocks & hardened glass make him feel
comfortable, though being locked inside
with Winchester rifles has him tinfoiling

his bedroom — he asks one of us but we're
getting ready for seeding & can't spare a moment.
Ring-necked parrots sit in the fruit trees

& he asks if they're famous. But he
doesn't talk much (really). Asked about Marilyn
he shuffles uncomfortably — outside, in the

spaces between parrots & fruit trees
the stubble rots & the day fails
            to sparkle.

Bluff Knoll Sublimity

for Tracy

1.

The dash to the peak anaesthetises
you to the danger of slipping as the clouds
in their myriad guises wallow about
the summit. The rocks & ground-cover
footnotes to the sublime. The moods
of the mountain are not human
though pathetic fallacy is the surest
climber, always willing
to conquer the snake-breath
of the wind cutting over
the polished rockface,
needling its way through taut
vocal cords of scrub.

2.

It's the who you've left behind
that becomes the concern as distance
is vertical and therefore less inclined
to impress itself as separation; it's as if you're
just hovering in the patriarchy
of a mountain, surveying
the tourists — specks on the path
below. Weather shifts are part of this

[74]

and the cut of sun at lower altitudes
is as forgiving as the stripped
plains, refreshingly green at this time
of year. You have to climb it because it's
the 'highest peak' in this flat state,
and the 'you have to' is all you
can take with you as statement
against comfort and complacency:
it's the vulnerability that counts up here.

3.

You realise that going there to write a poem
is not going there at all, that it's simply
a matter of embellishment, adding
decorations like altitude,
validating a so so idea
with the nitty gritty of conquest.
Within the mountain another
body evolves — an alternate
centre of gravity holding
you close to its face.
From the peak you discover
that power is a thick, disorientating
cloud impaled by obsession, that
on seeing Mont Blanc — THE POEM —
and not Mont Blanc — THE MOUNTAIN —
the surrounding plains
with their finely etched topography
can be brought into focus.

Skeleton Weed/Generative Grammar

(i) Finite-state

The 'i' takes in what is said —
yes, it is easily led
across the floors of discourse
only to find itself a force
easily reckoned with: there's
no point in stock-taking arrears
as fleshly interests tell you
nothing except acceptability & taboo.
Take skeleton weed infesting
the crop — rosette of basal
leaves unleashing a fatal
stem with *daisy-like* flowers
that drop (into) parachute clusters
of seeds. One missed when
they scour the field (men
& women anonymously-clothed
seated on a spidery raft dragged
behind a plodding tractor,
monotony testing the free-will factor),
can lead to disaster.

(ii) Phrase-structure

{[((analyz)ing)] [the ((constituent)s)]}
we examine(?) the wool of sheep
for free-loading skeleton-weed seeds,

their teeth specifically designed
for wool: the ag department
have decided they ARE selective
though admit our investigations
will help their 'research'.

(iii) transformational

One year the farmer asked us if we
felt guilty for missing one & hence ruining
his would-have-been bumper crop.
Quarantined the following year. Losing
his unseeded would-be bumper crop.
Ruining his credit rating. His marriage.
His son's & daughter's places
at their exclusive city boarding
schools. His problem with alcohol.
His subsequent breakdown
& hospitalization. (?) We remained
& still remain passive. Still we remained
& remain passive. But we [look(ed)] deeply,
collectively & independently
into our SELVES. Our silence
was an utterance of a loud inner speech.
A loud inner speech was an utterance
of our silence. Speaking for myself,
I've included in my lexicon of guilt
the following: what I feel today
will I feel tomorrow? And those tight
yellow flowers: so beautiful on the wiry
structures they call 'skeleton weed'.

Brothers Trapping Parrots at Mullewa

Using an old bed base
propped in one corner
with a star picket
and sprung with a length
of cable from behind
the superphosphate shed,
two brothers
with the blessing
of their father
trapped flocks
of pink and grey galahs,
red and black tailed
cockatoos and Port
Lincoln parrots,
to take back
to city aviaries.
That these birds ripped
the flesh of their fingers,
themselves suffered pernicious
injuries, and eventually
perished in damp hessian sacks
slung in a boot and carried
four hundred miles,
didn't cross the brothers' minds
as the flocks winged into view,
moved with a unitary stealth
towards the plump yellow grain

spread over ground compressed
by dual-wheeled tractors
and semitrailers
with wheels taller
than children
older than themselves,
as they whipped the star picket
from its leverage,
sealed their consciences
with adrenalin.
Those dank sacks,
those birds looking
like tea-tree rubbed back
by cattle and sheep.
The look on their mother's
face, a storm mixed
and primed in Mullewa,
brought to Perth
in the boot of a car.

Hydraulics, Flywheels, Saw and PTO

A regressive hiss settles pneumatics,
tightening coils of hoses, compressed
and ready to spring like snakes

disturbed from famished winter sleeps.
The mouthpieces fizz, oil saliva
coating the gauges, gulping its stale breath

and smoking black against the white frost
when the going gets tough, convulsing
about the hot connections, the motor idling

and teasing the pressure. The flywheel
warming under the slippage, the belt
pulled back by the saw's hunger for wood,

mallee root singing on the sawhorse,
flesh deep-bitten and screeching like a wounded
galah, the PTO turning for the hell of it,

a tail excited and impatient, keeping pace
with the hydraulics, flywheel and saw,
spinning furiously, without hindrance.

The Ascension of Sheep

The sun has dragged
the fog away
and now the sheep
in sodden clothes may

fleece the farmer —
who warm by the fire
tallies heads and prices
and thinks about slaughter —

each soul taken upwards
from its fertile
body — columns of mist
like pillars of a temple.

Come midday they'll
have dried right through
and follow the trail
down to the dam

where the water
refills the empty chamber
where the soul
could never feel secure.

Hoppers and Gargoyles

A screw drives the lupins towards the chute,
lupins spill into the hopper, an auger drags
them upwards towards the spout, lupins spill
into the silo. These are the facts, or facts
as they seem to the farmer who follows
the tried-and-true procedure, believes
what his eyes tell him, and is satisfied
with the end result. These are the facts
as his father has told him, neighbours confirm.

Another view, another set of facts: the gargoyle
masquerading as a spout draws all into its mouth
and spits it back, the hopper — its belly — endlessly
fuelled by the reaper who, disguised as a farmer,
cannot be content with endless death, but rather
gains its pleasure from the neighbours who believe
what they tell the farmer, who stare at the spout
and see no more than lupins filling his coffers.

Rock Picking: Building Cairns

The spine is best kept straight —
the weight of granite will damage
vertebrae, stretch the spinal cord.
    Let the knees do the work,
legs levering the load from ground
to trailer dragged at a crawl behind
    the Massey Ferguson tractor.

Cairnwards we move over the paddock,
building these self-contained environments
for snakes, spiders, and bush-wise architects.
    Ground lost is ground gained,
these cairns are completely functional.
Satellite cities linked by machinery that's
    commuter friendly if unpredictable.

Rune stones carefully placed, oblatory,
offerings for local deaths — accidents at harvest,
on gravel roads, wild tractors overturning,
augers catching a hand and swallowing flesh.
    And deities only farmers know.

Dried lichen and sweat mix to cement a cairn.
The surface suppressing the glitter of quartz —
pink, rose, white, transparent. Sources of warmth
these repositories of micro-chip technology
(unharnessed) attract infra-red telescopics,
blood coursing through their Frankenstein

monster bodies, distracting the predator's weapon
as it roams in search of foxes and rabbits.
Cairns — where youths empty swollen bladders
drunkenly into the fissures and cast amber bottles
into cobwebbed abysses, where wild oats grow at
impossible angles and lure the sun into darkness.

As I rock pick I unravel these pictures and spread
them to all corners of the paddock. I coin phrases,
devise anecdotes, invest the ups and downs of my
life in these cairns constructed from the landscape's
    wreckage, place sheep skulls on summits.

Alone, I feed these rowdy cities the stuff
of my blisters, sign the structures with broken
fingers, convert plans to ash and scatter
    them about the foundations.
Softly softly I sing the ruins of our
pampered anatomies, draw strength from the
    harsh realities of empire building.

And following duskfall, the tractor
and trailer no longer visible, I climb
onto the motorbike and drape myself over
    the seat — a bag of bones
slung over the tray of an iron jinker.
As the tractor comes into focus the cairns
    retreat — pyramids of the outback.

A Rare Sight

The bird seen first time here
in forty years sings lightly
on the wire, you turn to touch
the shoulder of a friend
and turning back together
find nothing but sky
and wire trembling.

Harvest

1   PRAYERS AND CHARMS

Harry spits blood at his crops on the eve of harvest —
warding off rain, high winds, excessive heat.
Jack takes a look over his shoulder and shoots
a cockatoo, divining weather's
intensity from the cast of its feathers.
Sue and Mary, their neighbours, interpret the stars
and are no longer the butts of jokes
in the district, they've been too accurate over the last
few seasons — even the Anglican minister
who puts a few acres in each year cocks an ear
when the gossip brings their predictions
floating through town.
Jack, it should be mentioned, also carries an amulet —
a good luck charm that's really a brass ring
that's losing its colour, as if the brass has been painted
over rusty iron and has begun to peel.
And of course a good few say their prayers
or cross their fingers or practise
strange rituals they've told no one about.

2 Dry Weather

And the headers are rolling through the crops
like electric shavers, the cut clean as the stalks
are dragged into the comb and the heads ripped
away, quail and snakes dispersing, the sun
sealing the cuts with a coppery swathe, the drivers
adjusting their headphones as dust drills the windows.
Children who have just finished exams check moisture
levels and signal that it's okay to continue.

3 Harvest Bans

Fire danger extreme.
The harvest bans
have been broadcast
and spread by word
of mouth. The bins
are closed until
late in the day
but still the
'don't-give-a-damn'
brigade push their
machines — flints
kindling the tinder.

Last season
one of them
was caught out

when a comb
hit an outcrop
of quartz
and sparked,
ten thousand acres
of crop going up
before volunteer
firefighters,
neighbours,
and some from
fifty miles away,
could extinguish
the sulky, persistent
flames. Even the field bins,
chock-a-block with the day's
ill-gotten gains, exploded
like grenades lobbed
from high ground.

4   BINS

Come the thunder of trucks
grain will whisper
through the grids.

Come the thunder of trains
we'll start the conveyors
and drain the bins.

We'll spear and sample —
count foreign bodies
under the keen eyes
of farmers,

check for ergot
as their features
grow ridiculously large.

Come the thunder of trains
we'll spread the tarps
and couple the wagons.

Come the thunder of trucks
we'll watch field mice
flicker amongst the stacks.

5   THE SUNSHINE HARVESTER

There's a story behind that sunshine harvester
lodged amongst the twisted hands
of ruined harrows and the decayed teeth
of dingo traps. The owner's brother
had been pouring sacks of ungraded wheat
through its crazy teeth when the grain
like incense lulled his brain
and he fell deeply into the hopper,
into the header's violent breath.

6 VERANDAH AND WATERMELON

This year's wheat cheque
and a remarkable yield
on sand plain country
accompany slices
of watermelon
on the back verandah.
A daughter calculates
debt per equity ratio,
her brother listens
to the cricket score
on the radio.
A parrot drops
a set of nectarines
with its bolt-cutter beak
and the farmer doesn't
even move. His wife
looks nervously at
the rifle and waits.
More nectarines
and he doesn't seem
to care. What about
those markets? What's
happening with subsidies?
Went sixteen bags an acre
of sand plain country.
Well I'll be damned.

Counterpoint

Counterpointing the death of twenty-eight
parrots so named because their call comes
twenty-eight twenty-eight twenty-eight
which is seven on three times a scatter gun's
twelve-gauge call, dumped by the boxful
four days into the new year and awaiting
the bulldozer's shadowy blade. Maybe
they hung thickly about a farmer's fruit trees,
maybe they sported under the sprinkler
on his only patch of green lawn. Maybe.

Shootings

1

I collected makers' names
like stamps — Winchester, Browning, Sportco,
the more exotic Finnish and German brands.

Death was a fantasy
made real
in the bush enclaves
of my uncle's farm.

Vermin!
was the password
before touching
a gun.

2

My oldest cousin's heart
is not in it — shooting
parrots that is.

He's taking me
because I'm up
for the holidays
and hungry
for trophies.

We march out
past the dams,
past Sand Springs
and Hathaways,
and close in
on a stand
of York gums.
I take aim
at a pair
of '28s'
and drop one.
Its partner sits
twisting its head,
picking at a branch
and glancing
towards the ground.
I reload and take aim.
My cousin grips my arm
and points to the corpse
splayed on the ground,
tail cocked heavenward.
Something twists
in my stomach.
I am too young
to put a name to it.
I lower the gun
and turn for home.

3

When I was twelve
I walked all day
mid-summer
without water —
rifle slung
over my shoulder,
sun obscuring
those wicked crows
my targets
(too smart
to be shot
by a kid
who measures death
by the number
of bullets
left in a packet)
and nearly died
of sunstroke.

4

I've seen photographs
in a biscuit tin
that show young men
sitting on mounds
of rabbit carcasses.
Mounds as tall
as the young men
they support.

5

The last thing I shot
was a ram with a broken
neck. It had been hit
by a car. Through
the open sight
I measured its breath
and for once
looked death
straight in the eye.

6

Rabbits frustrate
large men
with high-powered
rifles.

The lack of more
exotic game
leads them to vent
their frustrations.

Rabbits aren't just shot.
And full moons
do induce madness.

7

Harvest time, and
between shifts
workers corner
a pair
of screaming
foxes
in a forty-four
gallon drum

a shotgun wedding
in a forty-four

the sun skylarking
as the bouquet of lead
rips the steel
with a fizz

the gossip columnists
decked out
in army fatigues.

8

My uncle once killed
sheep with a knife.
Then he turned to the gun.
Regardless, city children
waited for the bladder
to be sprung.
The dogs frantic
below the carcass.

9

I placed the barrel
of a gun with a hair-trigger
against my tongue
as an experiment.
Tea-tree scraped at the windows
and all hell broke loose
in the chicken run.
The fox I sought
dropped from the roof of the coop
and sat at my feet —
too close to shoot
it ran
straight through me.

10

Did it a favour —
it was a mangy specimen
anyway!

11

Stalking.
Wending your way through.
Like dropping a parrot
mid-flight.
Downwind you approach
your upwind life.
Smell yourself.
Fear stinks.

12

I empty the breech and drain the powder.
I break the sights and seal the barrel.
I renounce the hunt, the flesh, the kill.
I embrace the sting of a cold morning,
      the flight of the parrot, the bark
of the fox, the utility of the rabbit.

Essay On Myxomatosis

Fence hugging I steer the car
down past the shed, the electric
rip of comb or cutter on abrasive
paper suppressing the roll of the frenetic
engine. The track heaves and shuffles,
rises and falls, rolls and dips
as slowly I approach the fading creek.
A shadow swallows the bonnet, I ease
to a stop and slip into neutral,
engaging the handbrake. A great
wedge-tailed eagle settles
in the stubble and starts to
lunge with prehistoric movements
towards a point between car and creek,
one eye on the car, the other on a rabbit
that has appeared on the track.
I open the door and lift myself out
of the seat. The eagle hesitates,
its beak agape like a gargoyle longing
for rain after drought. The rabbit
weaves tightening circles, the sun
blends with haze and shimmer,
a triangle of hunter and hunted,
the curious, afraid, and determined.
The rabbit stops. I draw closer.
The eagle braces its wings like a sail
ripped out of calm waters by storm winds,

spearing sight between us. The rabbit
turns towards me. Its eyes tumorous,
swollen. It targets me blindly, turns
towards the eagle which drops its wings
and lifts softly, tacking into the breeze,
its tension dispersed over the bronze
field, evaporating, eroding the song
of the grinder.
                The rabbit moves slowly
into the field, reading the braille
of pasture, its head rising and falling
with the tide of stubble.

The Silo

Visitors, as if they knew, never remarked
on the old silo with its rammed earth walls
and high thatched roof, incongruous amongst
the new machinery and silver field bins.
Nor the workers brought in at harvest time,
trucks rolling past the ghostly whimperings,
snarls and sharp howls cutting the thick silo's
baffling. Nor when a bumper harvest filled
every bin and the farmer was hungry
for space — no one ever mentioned bringing
the old silo back into service. This
had been the way for as far back as could
be remembered. Thin sprays of baby's breath
grew around its foundations, while wedding
bouquet sprouted bizarrely from the grey
mat of thatching. The sun had bleached the walls
bone-white while the path to the heavily
bolted door was of red earth, a long thin
stream of unhealthy blood. Before those storms
which brew thickly on summer evenings
red-tailed black cockatoos settled in waves,
sparking the straw like a volcano, dark
fire erupting from the heart of the white
silo, trembling with energy deeper
than any anchorage earth could offer.
And lightning dragging a moon's bleak halo
to dampen the eruption, with thunder

echoing out over the bare paddocks
towards the farmhouse where an old farmer
consoled his bitter wife on the fly-proof
verandah, cursing the cockatoos, hands
describing a prison from which neither
could hope for parole, petition, release.

Mala In Se: Death Of An Innocent By Snakebite

Mala prohibita or *mala in se*? The snake bites
and withdraws undetected. Death comes quietly
some hours later, an assumed thorn penetration
becomes a major oversight. Three weeks back a young
girl died in just this way on a neighbouring property,
an examination of her vital fluids revealing the venom.

In weighing the heart against the feather a trace of venom
will upset even the roughest of scales, the truth bites
the axis, destroys the balance, claims its property.
So, struck down in the hay shed, youth goes quietly,
taking its time over dinner and television, the young
in body and mind ignoring death's subtle penetration.

It shouldn't be allowed, they say, this penetration
of our lives — it's said by parent and doctor, the venom
tilting the balance in favour of *mala prohibita*. The young
girl's sisters are most vocal in this — living the bites
of snakes *in-stigmata*, cursing thorns as advocates. Quietly
time will soften bitterness and life return to the property.

But this, the fourth week since death claimed its property,
has not brought release. A red sun's harsh penetration
has not prevented an early winter falling quietly
though surely over paddocks, as fog in gullies, a venom
that is almost light and thin though deadly. Heat bites
like frostbite, the crow's glare destroys its young.

[103]

Mala in se someone actually mentioned — respect the young
came the reply (it was when the fallen girl's property
was being divided between her sisters). A tear bites
a stranger's flesh more than the knife — the penetration
of words well attested. So *mala in se* became a venom
more toxic than that of the snake. So, speak of it quietly.

We sit with the family on the ivy-clad verandah, quietly
discussing death and a cold sunset, the evening is young
though already a heavy darkness has set; but there is no venom
in the speech — acceptance from somewhere deep in the property
is slipping in: the call of crow and galah is penetration
enough to break bitterness. Cold though — even acceptance bites.

So quietly the soul retreats, no longer the property
of a sadness unwilling to release: the young soul's penetration
of *mala prohibita*'s venom. The lightness (*mala in se*) bites.

Why They Stripped the Last Trees
from the Banks of the Creek

They stripped the last trees
from the banks of this creek
twenty years ago. The old man
couldn't stand the thought
of bare paddocks with a creek
covered by trees slap bang
in the middle of them.
A kind of guilt I guess.
Anyway, he was old
and we humoured him —
chains, rabbit rippers,
chainsaws. We cleared
those banks until the water
ran a stale sort of red.
Until salt crept into
the surrounding soaks.
Furious he was — the salt
left lines on the bath,
the soap wouldn't lather.

Fog

For all its lymphatic nature
fog appears rapidly and spreads
its shroud tightly about the farm.

And though blinding, sheep and people
stumble smoothly through its unguent
body. Wood smoke fails to coerce

its opacity and drops moistly.
Apparently sectile it flinches
though heals instantly.

You drink its flesh with every breath.
Settling on low ground it climbs
to the peaks of hills and spills,

using trees and granite outcrops
as hungry boards. A submariner,
I walk the ocean's floor.

The fog thickens about the family
graves, tarnishing plaques
and chilling icons to the bone.

Finches zip like apparitions,
the sun, a limp beacon, drifts
to the rim of the system.

I mark the blurred silver
of a galvanised tank
as a point for navigation

and set off through the red flesh
of failing saltbush, over a carpet
of mustard she-oak needles.

The ground sinks and thickens.
In this quasi-world I hesitate —
as the fog burns my skin I sense

a fire's shadow and hear water
crackling as it fuels the mass
of liquid flame. A living entity

the fog, accepts me — I move steadily
on, confident that I will emerge
without a mark on my body.

Alf Reckons Lucy's The Bloke

Alf reckons Lucy's the bloke.
'She's the one with the balls,'
he says spitting into the cattle
grid.
        'Yeh, I reckon Lucy's the bloke.
That Anna's like my missus — always
complaining but big-hearted and goddamn
nice to the children. Stays at home.
That Lucy — Christ, she ploughs
and seeds and waters the stock.
She handles a header as well
as Geoff, myself, or Jock.
You've got to hand it to her.
Yeh, I reckon Lucy's the bloke.'

The Wild West

While drinking in the saloon bar
of a country hotel — pumping
the jukebox, liquored up
and making wisecracks — a gang
of bikers pulled up en masse
and hitched their bikes
to the street posts, horse rails.
A Valiant, laden with spare parts
and grog, covered the leading flank.
Filling the bar they told us
to piss off and shut our mouths.
I asked one of them where he'd
got his tats — he replied
with a stare as cold as his beer.
They drank from the jug, rolled joints,
throttled on amphetamines, swaggered
like gunfighters and petrol heads.
We slipped into the public bar
and watched over the shoulders
of locals who stared with kinked eyes
and mumbled into the gibbering
froth of their beers. The barmaid
kept the liquor flowing ('give 'em
enough rope'). The local cop
stood arms crossed, eyes fixed,
counting mug shots, smashed jugs.
We left for an hour or so. Returning,

a pool cue flew past our faces — 'Hey
you, could I borrow your nose!'
And then it snapped — one of the locals,
a fox-shooting, hay-bale-chested yokel,
kicked a Harley and guffawed as the pack
fell like the dominoes he'd seen
in newsreels at primary school. Within
seconds he was sprawled broken limbed
over the pavement. There were cops
everywhere — reinforcements had been
gathering on the outskirts of town
and were moving in. The bikers
saddled up, flicking a couple
of cops through the butcher's
window in the process. The law
retreated and formed a line
at the far end of the street.
The bikers spread out on their
revving Harleys. We stood in between.
The stand-off lasted two or three minutes.
The cops waited, the bikers waited.
And then on a signal from the Valiant
the bikers peeled off in pairs
and rode the gambit, lurching drunk
and heavy through the cordon
and into darkness, the Valiant
fishtailing behind them.

The Fire in the Forty-Four

We're broke this week so my brother
collects aluminium cans and the copper
insides of old hot-water systems —
you need sacks of aluminium
cans to make even a few bucks
but a few kilos of copper or brass knocks
the price right up. It's dusk
as we approach the metalman behind his sooty mask,
storm clouds tinged crimson
and sitting low over his sheet-iron
shed, an almost virulent fire
sparking up in the pit of a forty-four
gallon drum. His sons pour
acetylene into the wounded guts
of a truck, like lightning putting to rights
damage done in some long past storm.
Outside a load of scrap looks almost warm
as it awaits the furnaces of the city.
Our metal is hooked in sacks to scales painfully
close to the fury of the drum.
To the pain of heat the metalman seems numb.
Though as he swings the singed sacks aside
before they burst into flame I note him hide
a softness behind his gauntlets of calluses,
the delicate timing, the dexterity as he tallies
payment rapidly on bone-black fingers.
A flurry of rain hisses deep in the drum

and spits back at the storm.
The metalman speaks in tongues to his Vulcan
sons, who, deep in their alchemy, acknowledge only
with jets of flame. Quickly
he pays out and I follow my brother as he turns
away from the shed's darkening outline.

Goading Storms out of a Darkening Field

Goading storms out of a darkening field,
Cockeyed bobs seeding the salt, the farmer
Cursing the dry, cursing the bitter yield.

And while lightning would savage him with skilled
Thrusts, and floods strip the topsoil, it's better
Goading storms out of a darkening field

Than sit distraught on the verandah, killed
By the 'quitter's syndrome' — it's much safer
Cursing the dry, cursing the bitter yield.

Field bins empty, coffers bare, should have sold
Two years back when prices were halfway there.
Goading storms out of a darkening field.

Red harvest, charred hills, dry wells filled and sealed.
Sheep on their last legs. Dams crusted over.
Cursing the dry, cursing the bitter yield.

It's tempting when prayers and patience have failed,
Diviners have lost track of ground water.
Goading storms out of a darkening field.
Cursing the dry, cursing the bitter yield.

Parrot Deaths

1

Parrot deaths aren't mentioned
on this stretch of road, especially
in summer when vast scoured

fields leave only trees on the road,
long thin shadows that sprout rosellas
and twenty-eights in families,

when foliage is the emerald green
of chests exploding their small fists
against the windows of the car.

2

Or cracked under the wheel
spread-eagled, the sharp skull crack,
auguring spilt grain

from the gravel or brief stretches
of asphalt, harvesting the write-offs,
the contractors thumping their trucks

over the potholes and corrugations
on their way to the silos. Either gold,
orange, or blood-red sunsets erase death.

3

U-turn or reverse, scrape the red breast
of a rosella into the palm of your hand.
From here it's only a matter of moments

before breath suspends its downward slide,
brief glance of startled wonder,
the head lapsing into the swings

of a slow pendulum. Its wise-cracking beak
a husk for the salted kernel of its tongue,
still too tight to let death loose.

The Coconut Story

when the old man found the coconut
the coconut with no eyes found in the cemetery
he kept it & soon found a cousin's stolen stuff
& said the coconut will sort it out

the coconut with no eyes found in the cemetery
told Mancep — the magic man — the thief will return it
& said the coconut will sort it out
but tell no one or the magic will be undone

told Mancep — the magic man — the thief will return it
the coconut without eyes sees everything & speaks truth
but tell no one or the magic will be undone
the coconut expects those helped to give something back

the coconut without eyes sees everything & speaks truth
so the owner of the islands hears this & wants the coconut
the coconut expects those helped to give something back
but the owner wants to take the power away for himself

so the owner of the islands hears this & wants the coconut
Mancep says this is not the will of the coconut
but the owner wants to take the power away for himself
Mancep says a great disaster will come his way

Mancep says this is not the will of the coconut
though the owner takes it over the seas with him
Mancep says a great disaster will come his way
though for six years they hear nothing

though the owner takes it over the seas with him
he cannot control the power for the power is great
though for six years they hear nothing
& the people think the power has gone with him

he cannot control the power for the power is great
& he dies & his family brings the body back
& the people think the power has gone with him
because there is trouble & discontent everywhere

& he dies & his family brings the body back
though a great storm wrecks the ship
because there is trouble & discontent everywhere
because in the coffin was the coconut which the sea frees

though a great storm wrecks the ship
Mancep sees the coconut washed up on the beach
because in the coffin was the coconut which the sea frees
for Mancep to take back & set things right.

A Short Tour of the Cocos Atoll

From Rumah Baru the runabout
skips over the rippling tidal sweep,
the lift & drop of the hull's skin
like the crack of a sail full blown,
dead, full blown again. We traverse
sinkholes cool with depth,
almost black, like inverted islands
set in intertidal reef,
a sub-surface map
where intensity of colour
makes do for sonar.
Ashore on Pulu Labu —
the sheet anchor claws the sand,
a few chickens idle nearby.
On the island's ocean side
I lacerate my feet on splintered coral,
collect a composite rubber sheet
from which a dozen pairs of children's
thongs have been pressed somewhere
in Indonesia, brought by the tides
& currents to Cocos. A brown booby
glides high overhead,
the humid atmosphere
muffling its call — these birds
nest on North Keeling
which is out of reach, but are treasured
by the Cocos Malays as a 'delicacy',

a food for which the Federal police
will often travel to Home Island
to investigate a rumoured feast.
Jeff is busy casting a net
for bait fish, he hauls
in a small school & collects
the anchor. I squirm with the fish:
they flick at my feet as I grip
the gunwale. Jeff
steers towards Pulu Kembang
& I can tell he's
checking me out — test
the weird vegetarian
who lets fish go & loves
the orange & black concertinaed
bodies of sea-slugs, who
jumps onto the reef & tows
the runabout with unnaturally long legs.
The tide's retreat is in full swing.
We anchor a couple of ks from the beach.
Mud crabs bubble just below the flat.
Stands of driftwood lurk like booby traps.
Jeff chases reef sharks in knee-deep hollows
& tries to beach them. Their black tips race
towards dry land & dart suddenly
back to the depths. They are quicker than Jeff.
We walk to the island & walk back again.
The sun devastates our skin.
We suffer mutually.
Jeff heads for deep water

& says he wants to spear the treasured green fish.
He dives like a wounded frigate
& returns with nothing.
He is popular on Home Island
& speaks with thirty years
behind him. He is not the West Islander now.
And this is how I like him.
Returning to Rumah Baru
I wonder if he's the man the Cocos Malays
have been seeing — or almost seeing — shadowing
the coconut groves. Appearing at special moments,
bringing good luck.

West Island Report

It's little wonder the Home Islanders
want to keep this mob off their island.
Drinkers living in each other's pockets
with a language all their own.
Even those on short tours —
which often become shorter tours —
pick up a kind of addled Strine.
They work on 'Cocos Time',
wear as little as possible,
& look forward to the charter
jet's arrival. They form societies
that parody the mainland & drink duty-free
liquor at the Club. *Rumour* is their neighbour
so most aspire to owning a boat —
getting out into the ocean
where they can't be seen — the irony
of a small community in isolation.
West Island with its land & ghost crabs,
bantam chooks darting in & out
of the coconut palms. Its Sydney highway
as thin as a fanbelt & a whole 7 ks long,
the high-pitched drone of ex-postal bikes
& nights out in the Cocos Lodge Mess.
Mick, husband of Ali (sometimes
secretary to visiting writers),
is a great cook who dreams
of setting up in a posh restaurant

on the mainland. Ali misses Kenya
but loves the life on Cocos.
They also have a boat & like a drink.
Hosai cooks a good chilli dish.
His chillies are grown hydroponically
at West Island's very own
market garden. Lettuces the size of fists
grow there. But then in-micro
so do many other things.
But most people pay extra
to have fresh veges flown
up from Perth — broccoli
& cauliflower that look like coral.
Oh, the Club is also the cyclone shelter
so if things look really bad
like during the 1909 cyclone
which destroyed 90 per cent
of the coconut palms
& demolished most of the houses
on Home Island, then no doubt
most will hit the bar & die pissed.
The military make fleeting visits
but people don't speak
too much of these unless
they've had a few too many.
Don't forget, the girl next to you
at the pub might be one
of the hospital's nurses
& know more about you
than you think.

At the Quarantine Station
they keep sterile chooks
to warn of undetected
diseases. Lately ostriches
have been the go — Australians
& Canadians at each other's throats
over who owns the chicks. The Feds
are even taking an interest.
The Cocos Indus Malay
Restaurant has started
a fish & chip night.
A couple of kids have painted
the school walls. The feral dive shop
has closed early — Dieter, 'good bloke he is',
watches that tourists don't dive too deep.
And JCR, no longer the boss,
sells ornamental shells to the Japanese.
He's not such a bad bloke but won't tell
any secrets. The Cocos Malays
say he knows the spirits.
The West Islanders reckon
he holds the best parties
& tells great jokes.

Indian Ocean Ode

The long arms of a cyclonic nebula
whip coconut palms into a trance-like frenzy.
The remaining ironwood — stunted — cut back
for carvings, firewood, & boats —
snarls. Cabbage bush & pandanus
heave & shudder. Coral cays
suffer damage on the fringes,
the relentless assault of the seas
grinding the living tips
of the volcanic sea mount.
Heavy rain covers freshwater lenses
in their coral sand aquifers
like sets of contacts.
Even iron drums
filled with gelatinous
palm oil seethe, bubbles speaking
with a voice as syrupy as cholesterol.
Fish dive deep into sinkholes,
the lagoon froths & whinges
against the coral. Boats
break their moorings.

A bright morning makes a liar
of the water's dark orchestrations.
The loyalties of small communities
(linked only by slow-boats & slow-to-come
air-charters, where a population
gathers at the airstrip to see what's new
or drink themselves to death among

the tourists at the social club),
are sorely tested, all lines
of communication
being down.

The sky is clear
& below the ocean's surface
Moorish idols perform coralline
rituals. Parrotfish graze quietly.
The coral, in its atmosphere
of fish & anemones, univalved
& bivalved predators, rip & dart
of reef sharks, repairs itself
& builds outwards.
On the surface
signs of the cyclone
are everywhere — a tangled carpet
of palm leaves, household debris, & even
the leeward islands littered
with flotsam & jetsam.
Land crabs re-emerge
from the undergrowth
to devour new layers of leaf litter,
council workers & house owners
kick through the wreckage,
recaptured boats sail reefwards
where gorgonian fan corals
wave delicately
& the Indian Ocean settles
like amniotic fluid around
the *myth of origin*.

Anathalamion

My parents dead & the family property
broken up, I live on *their* place — in the old shearing
quarters — & keep an eye on things. Talking
business with the old man is impossible though the old lady
comes to the quarters once a week & we sit with a cuppa & study
the week's takings — sorting out the bills & tallying
the red & black figures. She's always been good
with numbers. But it's like she's given up caring
about things really — just working the sums to trade
away the bad memories. The old man sits in a hide
down by the creek some days — watching the blue heron
high in the red gum tree that was blasted
by lightning years back. When I go to the hotel
they ask me what the old couple do these days but I just get plastered
& stare into my beer — snubbing even the mayor — 'To Hell
with the lot of you!' I'll yell, just waiting for a quarrel.
On a dark day, when the season was closing in,
they were seen leaving the town, like the blue heron.

After their son's death the blue heron became the old man's
obsession and his wife told me he only ever spoke to her when
talking of them. The blue heron, their nest raided by crows, have
left the redgum this year. I like to think they're nesting nearby —
maybe further up creek where the redgums are still thick. Their
son had once claimed that he'd been told by a hay stooker that if
you died near a heron your soul joined with its soul. He'd told that
to his parents and they'd laughed. He marvelled that it was called

a blue heron when it was more of a grey colour. On a dark day, when the season was closing in, they were seen leaving the town, like the blue heron.

As children we'd burrow into the hay
or move bales like building blocks, trapping
carpet snakes. Together saw Tad Hunter clutching
at the mangled stump of his arm, the auger crazy
with his blood. Once we nearly drowned in a silo of barley,
sinking further with every move, pulled out crying
by his old man who said we'd learnt our lesson & didn't need
punishing any further. Who said the same, when — riding
his motorbike — we hit the cattle grid & skewed
into the creek. And when we fed a pet sheep his premium seed
wheat & watched it die from pickle poisoning. Neighbours
called us feral kids — 'little bastards, getting their claws
into everythin', like locusts in the crop, nothin' can stop
'em.' It's true, we ran amok, but we did our chores
& didn't mean any harm — a chip
off the ol' block his dad would say to the town cop.
On a dark day, when the season was closing in,
they were seen leaving the town, married again.

In some ways it was like a world under glass — porous glass that let in the creek and the birds and the weather and the children who'd creep up to the house as a dare, the old people having *that* reputation for strangeness, but kept the pain in, petrified in the moment. The boy's death had cut it off from the outside world and it existed in a twilight which not even the most determined seasons could breach. I never said much about him. I read a lot and kept to myself. But even the brightest books seemed dull. The shadows of the blue heron indelible on their pages. On a dark day, when the season was closing in, they were seen leaving the town, like the blue heron.

It was one of those days when the black
cockatoos were low-loping in a storm-stained sky
& the creek ran river-thick, scouring the red clay
banks & swamping the nests of water rats, & the track
up to the top gate was up to the axles with mud & a long trek
around the flooded paddocks was necessary, stray
sheep stuck firm, the silos damp & full of sprouted wheat,
that they both emerged in black raincoats & doggedly
made their way to town on foot. As word had spread, the main street
was lined with adults & children who thought they were in for a treat.
But the old couple didn't lift their heads, & neither led
the other as they marched like mourners or a parody of the dead,
marching a slow funereal slog towards the empty church.
A few moments later the priest appeared
& followed them into the silence beyond the arch.
On a dark day when the season was closing in,
they were seen leaving the town, married again.

*Note: 'blue heron' is a local nickname for the 'white-faced heron' –
a bird that is largely blue-grey.*

Lightning Tree

It's stark white in this hard
winter light. At its base
brackish water spreads like exposed film
out through marsh grass & paperbarks —
a snapped bone, it punctures the skin.
On its splintered crown
the Great Egret stretches, its knifed beak
piercing the cold blue sky —
an inverted lightning strike
fielding its wings —
a crucifix — hesitating,
as if held by a magnet,
then dropping into flight,
dragging lightning rod legs.

In Expectation of a Lightning Strike
on Wireless Hill

In expectation of a lightning strike
On Wireless Hill you sit and wait — a Passover
Sky brooding like tinfoil in smoke-bush —
Charged and ready to tap into the suburbs.
When asked where birds go during a storm
You can answer that it's here —
To this hill: cockatoos and rosellas
Clustering in the lower limbs of banksias
And eucalypts. You say to yourself
That this visit is purely scientific,
That it's *likely* a strike
Will happen here — the highest
Ground for miles around.
The road that rings the hill
Is like a black echo renewing
Its pulse towards extinction —
Like a rare species of flower rekindled
After having been 'lost forever'.
So you sit, earthed by observation and conjecture,
In expectation of a lightning strike
On Wireless Hill.

Tremors: A Report

Some of us live willingly on fault-lines.

'An earthquake which swept across the southern half of W.A. at
11 a.m. yesterday flattened the wheat-belt town of Meckering
(population 250), 84 miles north of Perth.'
                                        − *West Australian*, 15 October, 1968

Eighty-four miles south of Meckering the metronome skipped a beat
                    & wandered across the piano,
paintings tilted & dried paint dripped to the floor. McCubbin's bushman
                    lost a billy full of hot, strong tea.
We rushed from the house as the ground rippled like a mirage, or
heat waves on the road. My mother gripped my arm hard enough
                    to drive dark crescents deep
into flesh. Trees trembled while birds sat perfectly still,
as if balanced on gyroscopes. The dog cowered on the porch.

Pipes burst, houses collapsed, roads erupted, paddocks were
torn apart, railway tracks became fluid & whipped out like dugites
    sunning themselves on beds of warm blue metal, silos cracked —
    feed grain running like rivers through the openings — parrots,
strangely silent before the quake, clustered like emerald jewels
on the yellow halo about the ruins, gullies opened, chicken coops
were sprung, water tanks torn — their precious contents drained
    through shattered crusts of salt. Bridges blocked suddenly
                    empty creeks.

Townsfolk, it is said, hid under sinks & tables & stood in door-
frames. The Civil Defence Service, CWA, & Red Cross went straight
into action. Tea & blankets & the chant *our town is no more
let us rebuild our town is no more let us rebuild* which had the air
of a mantra when droned in the wide-open spaces. And later their
self-admonition *there had been tremors but we chose to ignore
them there had been tremors but we chose to ignore them*
which gradually became *there'd been tremors but we'd had them
before there'd been tremors but who would have thought*. Though
some wags from the Cunderdin Gliders' Club joked that it would
have been safer riding thermals than turbulence on the
stormy *terra firma*.

Wheatlands was only seven miles from the epicentre. The walls
of the homestead fractured, paddocks opened, the surrounding hills
convulsed. Auntie Elsie, custodian over the original Wheeler
Homestead, watched as her house sank. Later she'd joke that its
tilt was like the Leaning Tower of Pisa. My cousins slept in their
car overnight. Afterwards, they found that dry wells had filled with
water, freshwater wells
had run dry or turned salt, soaks flooded into gullies, thickly-
walled earthen dams had split & emptied out onto the paddocks
carrying saplings like driftwood, that fences had been uprooted —
wire snapping like overwound clock springs, that straw-thatched
barns had become stooks in the houseyard. The horses were crazy
for days & the chooks wouldn't lay. The York church held extra
services & there were special collections for those hardest hit.
At school the kids were full of it.

They've built a gazebo as memorial in Meckering. The Meckering
Agricultural Society (Inc) has brought out a souvenir booklet
full of maps, notes, & photographs. They've rebuilt the town
      three hundred metres south — imperial has long since
given way to metric — out of tin & steel-reinforced concrete. There
is a fledgling tourist industry. Everybody you talk to refers to the
      silence of the birds on the morning before the quake.
They seem to need to talk with outsiders. Hadn't even seen a bird
that morning, a man balanced on a bicycle adds. His wife had called
      it a storm beneath the ground. That it'd been like wading
                        through heavy surf. That people
had lost everything except ridiculous items like curtain fittings. That
they'd suffered complete derangement of the senses while the earth
was erupting. Date palms mark the site of the old town. There is
      a memorial plaque & a pair of garden lions that feign vigilance.
Apparently there are up to five hundred tremors each year,
though only a few are felt — these rattle crockery & unsettle orn-
      aments. Some of the older residents believe it is the unsteady
hand of the old lady who died of fear after the quake — assuring
herself that family dinner sets & nostalgic bric-a-brac are real,
      not fragments mingled with dust in the ruins of her house.

Approaching the Anniversary of
my Last Meeting with my Son

I never write 'confessional' poetry
but your voice — like forked lightning
etching a thunder-dark river — leaves me
no choice but to speak directly.
I hear your mother laugh.
That I've screened myself
in the ash of burnt images,
left nothing intact behind.
It's almost the anniversary
of my leaving, and you don't
know my voice on the phone
when you ring Nanna.
Told it's Daddy,
you say, 'I'd better go,'
your mother erupting
from another room;
it's not safe using the phone
during a storm. And peace
is as important at home
as food and warmth, so I let it go.
Sometimes I sit on Deep Water Point jetty
and remember the time we spent
considering what lies below
the glistening surface,
what drives mottled brown jellyfish
in scattered flotillas

to beach themselves,
why herons strut their stuff
curious yet suspicious —
having to answer to no more
than the weather,
small fish, and an urge to be free.

Tenebrae

for Tracy

You are on the verge
of a resurrection,
standing on a fragile shoreline,
erosion undermining
the limestone cliff face,
expecting to plunge suddenly
into the churning ocean.
You'd rebuild memories,
though this coastline
is always changing — a childhood
hiding place eroded,
an overhang collapsed
like the tide. Those
limestone columns
reaching towards a god
that would take your past
as if it were an offering.
But though the lights
one by one extinguish
as you explore deeper,
that final light — the sun —
grows stronger,
despite the coming winter,
the darkening seas.

Wild Radishes

Across the dark fields the family is spread
While overhead the sky is haunted,
In the dull light they scour the crop
Never looking up as the day seems to stop.
Wild radishes missed will destroy the yield —
Bills to be paid, deals to be sealed.
But the plover's refusal to lift and drop,

And the absence of crow and parrot talk,
And the immense racket as stalk rubs on stalk,
Registers somewhere deep in the soul.
And as the sun begins to uncoil —
The deep green of the wheat uneasy with light —
The golden flowers of wild radishes bite
Just before they are ripped from the soil.

Drowning in Wheat

They'd been warned
on every farm
that playing
in the silos
would lead to death.
You sink in wheat.
Slowly. And the more
you struggle the worse it gets.
'You'll see a rat sail past
your face, nimble on its turf,
and then you'll disappear.'
In there, hard work
has no reward.
So it became a kind of test
to see how far they could sink
without needing a rope
to help them out.
But in the midst of play
rituals miss a beat — like both
leaping in to resolve
an argument
as to who'd go first
and forgetting
to attach the rope.
Up to the waist
and afraid to move.
That even a call for help

would see the wheat
trickle down.
The painful consolidation
of time. The grains
in the hourglass
grotesquely swollen.
And that acrid
chemical smell
of treated wheat
coaxing them into
a near-dead sleep.

Echidna

for Jacques Derrida

Rhythmically burrowing up on the top road
in the graded remainders, the swampy contours
that look good for digging, that you'd
like to get amongst and smell —
those substrata, more than dirt and roots,
rhizomic agendas of the feeble-eyed,
uttering up refrains from where
compactness and density
are demarcation and territory,
where decaying mallee root
or corpse of storm-felled wandoo
tan the leathery bag of muscled fluid,
the flow of ants as white as Moby Dick,
as determined against the pulpy hull of trees
as against the gridded surface. Down where
the highway is sensed in the movement of sand-
particles, the *hérisson* — *istrice* in Italian,
in English, hedgehog — excavates
determinedly. At risk, this bristling heart
litters the roads with dedication,
symbols of the national psyche
left to bloat in the sun's blistering
prosody: *inseparation* that mimes
mechanics on the surface: *<by heart>*,

that without footnotes is still recognised
as the source of all under-movings.
I consider as memory tracking an echidna
with a farmer in jam tree country —
locating the spirit of place,
as if its being curled in a tree hollow
might validate the vast spread
of open tillage — but struck
by a kind of amnesia we wandered
in a circle tight as a fist, exhuming
the deeply choric question of rendering
our meanderings into prose,
into idle chatter to accompany
a few beers in the pub that night;
the portfolio of our imagined data
presented with detachment
as the slow-moving underminer
of our confident lyrical selves
fed ravenously,
deep in the heart
of the forest.

The Hunt

for Les Murray

A bounty of 'fame throughout the district and no
chores for a week' was placed on The Tiger by my
        Uncle. We'd all seen it
        plenty of times over
the years — a huge beast that came down from the Top Bush
and raided the chicken coop, took the guinea fowl,
        and slaughtered pets. It was
a true feral, begotten by ferals. It was,

in a sense, a species entire in itself.
Those many sightings over the years of a 'large
        predator' we put down
        to The Tiger. It seemed
like a joke of nature — green-grey fur with musty
yellow waves running like stripes down its flanks, massive
        jaw with steel teeth that shone
as it snarled in a spotlight before vanishing

into the bush. For two years it had been hunted —
even the local pro fox shooter couldn't bring
        home its scalp. One winter
        holidays my cousin
and I packed our tent and kit, shouldered arms and crossed
into the scrub. Deep into the dark forbidding

foliage we plunged. We struck
camp close to the centre
of the island of wandoo and mallee, a large

copse surrounded by florescent green crops of wheat.
At dusk we shot three grey rabbits as they emerged
from their warrens. It was
quick and nothing was said.
Placing them in a damp hessian sack we spent hours
traipsing through the bush by torchlight, dragging the sack
behind us. The scent spread,
we emptied the corpses
on a patch of open ground and set to digging

hollows and laying traps — fierce iron jaws decayed
by rust, straining beneath sand-covered newspaper
disguising the ambush.
We took turns in laying
them, one holding the torch, the other spiking chains
into dirt, bracing springs with a boot. The traps ringed
the offering. Rubbing
the ground with a corpse we masked our sharp scent before

casting it back on the pile. The cold bit at our
bones. Finished, we didn't linger — a strange fear took
hold of us and something
nudged its way under our
confidence. We returned to the campsite. Morning
was bitter — tamarisks were heavy with frost, sheathed
with rapiers of ice.

We struggled with a fire,
ate by the smouldering, eye-stinging hearth. Rifles

in hand we made our way to the place. *The Altar
of the Dead* one of us muttered without humour.
            The Tiger was there. Dead —
            frozen solid. The stripes
on its flanks blurred by the dark matting of fur. Three
of the traps had snatched its limbs; the others had been
            triggered and lay beaten
nearby. The Tiger had chewed off its trapped forepaw

which lay half-digested in the trap's maw, back legs
stretched as if by some medieval torturing
            device. The carcasses
            of the rabbits had not
been touched. We buried them with The Tiger; buried
the traps, deep. We packed our gear and went home, telling
            Uncle that The Tiger
            would never be caught, that
it was a creature not of this world — a bitter
cold had struck our bones, fire bringing no relief.

Reticulating the Avocados

Having sold off the top paddocks to finance
The overdraft, they looked to diversify.
The market price high, they took a chance

On avocados, being the first to defy
The recommended climatic conditions,
To plant despite the frosts and dry

Biting heat of the district — the frisson
Of succeeding against the odds
Driving them on despite derision

From locals who gave sarcastic nods
To each other in the town's main street
No doubt secretly afraid that the gods

Might in their fickleness choose to greet
The scheme with favourable reports
And bring avocados to their world of wheat

And sheep, nurture an enclave of foreign fruits.
But a dry place with a sun that burns
Even the toughest plants to the roots

Does not lend itself to altruistic turns
And will ignore even the blessings
Of the most sympathetic Dionysians.

So after preparing the soil to take each seedling
They created a second atmosphere
Beneath a field of shade cloth, unwinding

Rolls of plastic piping, hoping to auger
Water down from the dam, to feed
It through the network, to steer

Its life-giving properties to the orchard.
But despite the influence of gravity
The water refused to be drawn, the red

Soil that tainted the dams of the valley,
Weighed heavy in the pipes. Attaching
A pump they forced the slurry

Down onto the field, slowly flooding
The plot like the fertile plains
Of an alluvial delta. With nurturing

The trees grew slowly while the grains
Were harvested. Frosts and blight
Bit into their flesh and the tell-tale stains

Of fungus appeared on their skins. For all
These setbacks most of them bore
Fruit within four years. At first, a light

Crop, but then each year brought more.
The town talked about the prices they'd charge
For avocados in the fruit and veg store.

Gradually others saw the advantage
And began to plant using the same scheme.
Avocados became all the rage.

The Great Drought ended the dream.
The red water set solid in the pipes,
Arteriosclerosis choking the system.

An Aerial View of Wheatlands in Mid-Autumn

'Indeed, it is a question if the exclusive reign of this orthodox
beauty is not approaching its last quarter.'
    – Thomas Hardy, *The Return of the Native*

In the reciprocity of summer
And the year's first frosts, the green eruption
Hesitant, the stramineous remainder
Of last season's crop converts to nitrogen
As slowly overhead the spotter plane
Dissects the quickening flesh of Wheatlands,
The probing eye of the camera hidden
From your curious surveillance, while stands
Of mallee gnaw at the salty badlands.

They will offer to sell you the stolen
Moment, the frozen minutiae of your
Movement within the tableau, the tension
Extracted with such unwanted exposure:
The screams of the cockatoo, the tractor
Aching deep in its gut having swallowed
A brace of teeth as it crunched into gear,
Bleats of sheep on their way to be slaughtered,
The drift as a neighbour sprays weedicide.

Remember though that if given the chance
You would scrutinize someone else's yard,
So it may be worth adjusting your stance
In the light of such a double standard.
Forget that the land looks scarred and tortured:
That call for order in the rural scene,
For Virgil's countryside satiated
With weighty corn and Campanian wine,
And consumed by olives and wealthy swine,

Is not the harmony of this decade.
Instead look to the flux of soil and fire,
The low loping flight of the darkest bird,
The frantic dash of the land-bound plover,
The breaking of salt by errant samphire,
The flow of water after steady rain,
The everlasting in bright disorder,
The stealthy path of the predating plane
Cutting boundaries as you sow your grain.

The Journey

There was nothing else to do
but position the corpse
in the cabin — the back
of the ute
full of fencing gear
which his father
wasn't about to leave
out in the middle
of nowhere.
So he had to sit
in between like an apostrophe —
as if holding the soul
to the body.
'He's still pretty fresh —
I'd hazard a guess
that his heart packed
it in. What he was
doing out there
Hell only knows!
Waterless, and the sun furious!'
bellowed his father.
So he sat there as the corpse
stiffened, held to the seat
by the belt. He didn't look at it
once during the journey,
though could sense
the anger in his father

at having to go so far out of their way —
his thick sweat poisonous
as the ute
eroded those miles
into town.

Pig Melons

As children we dashed
their brains out,
the insipid flesh
drying like chunks of pork
over the yellowing paddocks;
this murder bringing
further ruin to arable lands,
choking the native flora
with spilt thoughts
encoded as seeds
that bided their time
spitefully
until the rains
washed away the tracks
of our games, our conflicts,
percolating beneath the surface,
throwing ropes
that crept out,
securing the meagre
fertility of the place
with their rituals
of bondage.

On the Transferring of Three Generations of Family Ashes from their Graves — A Farewell to Wheatlands

for Lorraine Wheeler

And the ashes will be lifted out of the loam
and carried to the foot of Mount Bakewell,
lifted out of the mummified flesh
of the farm, to await their new shape,
farm-bones showing through parched skin
scratched up by the random though determined
assaults of wind-flurries upside-downing
the ordnance, usurping maps
with strain and nervous tension,
harassing the labourers shovelling grain,
grimacing about the gargoyle-spouts of the silos
working on regardless, as if there's
something to this bullshit about 'cycles',
as if the repetition of drive-belts
and insistent circuits of pink and grey galahs
raucous over the Aztec accumulations
of mudbrick are *de rigueur*, as if this grave-plot
within its aging fence *is* the New World,
as if last year's harrowed ground
blackens round the rim like the fire-gutted
home of a family that left a long way back
because they'd no choice, because terraces

of termites are inevitable, their forms
rising and falling in the weirding grasses,
yellow in the thin waves of tainted summer,
each grave noted as a milestone
on the road to repetition, anonymity.
And the ashes will be lifted out of the loam
and carried to the foot of Mount Bakewell.

Each year Paterson's Curse decorates the farm
like kitsch — even during this savage dry
which must break soon. That in rich soil
mechanisms of purple flowers
drive to draw sunlight
to its awl, this weed that would
consume the fields, a cover-all
that plasters wounds inflicted
by ball & chain, the stain
that is the sun's unreturnable gift,
plovers charging burnished bones
of liveried beasts fallen in heaps
with the limitless summer.
And the ashes will be lifted out of the loam
and carried to the foot of Mount Bakewell.

Rose quartz sparkles about
a wandoo altar, a dugite's skin
mimicking the detritus of woodpiles
as the new owners check out the place
and wonder where it is they stand.
When the family first arrived they

reckoned it was theirs for the taking.
A gift from God. The shadows
were driven back into the trees,
where it was guessed they belonged.
And now the wide open fields
are both shadowless and treeless.
The place's name has been lost.
The territory remains
but with boundaries redrawn.
Later, they'll embrace beneath a tree
none of you had noticed before
and it will become *their* sacred place,
and be named accordingly.
And the ashes will be lifted out of the loam
and carried to the foot of Mount Bakewell.

A patch of fallen grain
lifts light in varicoloured
paddocks; and the people of the district,
for all their apparent crimes,
will get rid of you before
you get rid of them, and the smaller
their spread, their tractor, the truck
they've used for carting grain,
the more they'll remain and prosper.
And the ashes will be lifted out of the loam
and carried to the foot of Mount Bakewell.

The sun burns its wealth
into your skin until

[155]

you can't take any more
and stay indoors. Though
like all finite resources it pullulates
about the steady state
of your faith — but you can't
afford to drop the price
despite the state of fences and firebreaks
around the dams and gulleys.
And the ashes will be lifted out of the loam
and carried to the foot of Mount Bakewell.

And the old Chev truck that's sat
fixed like sculpture for thirty years
moves indiscernibly as a black-faced
cuckoo shrike twirls in a pepper tree,
or darts from machinery in the new shed
down to the river gums at the neck
of the salt, and old wells breathe
through cracks in railway sleepers
or rusty sheets of corrugated iron.
The arteries beneath the farm
are indifferent to the polypipe's
mimicry, the pseudo songlines
of a temporary occupation.
And the ashes will be lifted out of the loam
and carried to the foot of Mount Bakewell.

The family has gathered for Christmas
and while the younger cousins
you spent your childhood with

clarify memory and *your* having been there,
the oldest cousin whose life
had little to do with yours
expresses surprise at your recall.
It's as if you were never part of it.
You point out that *he* hadn't 'been there' —
an older boy ignoring the 'kids'.
He's astonished when you remember
Gerry milking Princess the cow,
and that his horse Treasure,
frenzied by a lightning strike,
was found dead, hooked in a forked tree.
And he talks of the stubble being burnt —
strange ritual with his father
as master of the ceremony —
flames burning towards the centre,
eating each other's breath,
leaving the paddock black and indelible
and hungry for seed and nutrients.
And the ashes will be lifted out of the loam
and carried to the foot of Mount Bakewell.

The Machine of the Twentieth Century Rolls
Through the High-Yielding Crop

Dust particles cling to sweat despite the sun just up,
moisture levels within brittle stalks drop
as rapidly as markets are lost or gained, shadow
puppetry of information exchange leading the finest
of mechanical technologies astray, as over the crop

the machine of the twentieth century poises — straining
against dry dock, a *Titanic* that won't be sunk in those deepest
spots of abundance, a post-modern Ceres busy at the helm
lest a hidden rock break the fingers clawing in the grain;
this schizophrenic God whose speech is a rustle, a token bristling

like static on the stereo, despite state-of-the-art electronics
and a bathyspherical cabin of glass and plastic sealed
against all intrusion though retaining hawk-like vision and radio
contact with the outside world. On the fringes — at home base,
or by the gate — the workers are ready to launch out, to drain

grain from a bulging bin. The art of harvesting is in the hiding
of the operation. Behind clean lines and sun-deflecting paint
the guts of the machine work furiously; from point of entry
to expulsion the process is relentless — from comb working greedily,
grain spirals up elevators, thrashed in a drum

at tremendous speeds, straw spewed out back by
manic straw-walkers, the kernels falling to sieves below

as fans drive cocky chaff out into the viscous
daylight. The sun at mid-morning rages out of control,
glutted on this excess fuel. Melanomas spread on field workers

as they tarp a load; the driver plunges with precision
back into the crop, setting a perfect line, de-mystifying
this inland sea — an illusion, a mirage that hangs around
just before summer has reached full-blown. City granaries
filling, factories churning, 'design' a catchword instigating

plenty — the risks of intensive farming, tomorrow's worry —
stubble itching, high yields floating like oil on troubled waters,
the *Titanic*'s myth attracting the districts of the hungry.

A Bright Cigar-Shaped Object Hovers
Over Mount Pleasant

It starts in the park near Brentwood Primary School
and moves rapidly towards Mount Pleasant
a bright cigar-shaped object that darts
and jolts across the demarcation lines
of class that aren't supposed to exist in Australia
but do because even Labor voters prefer
to be on the Mount Pleasant side of the divide
if for no other reason than it pushes property
prices up. It follows the line of my escape-
route from school, the same route a man
without a face in a dark car crawls along,
calling to me as I break into a run,
the car door opening and a clawed hand
reaching out to drag me in, the cigar-
shaped object stopped stock still
and hovering like the sun, hovering
as if it's always been in that spot, always
been overhead, as hot as hell despite
the cold setting in, the sweat emanating
from my forehead, the light bright in my eyes.

Dispossession

Watson: Where do wicked people go at death?
Yeenar: To a very great fire I believe.
Watson: That is very bad, and is not to be trifled with.
Yeenar: Oh yes fire very good, very good.

— Journal of W. Watson, September 21 1834,
Church Missionary Society Records, AJCP

protection
aggravated
destruction
Almighty
construction
proclamation
probability
autonomy
disease
species
autonomy
links
quality
vis-à-vis
the centralised
London dealer in native art
landing
like something out of songlines
the press

commission/s
traditional
punishments
appropriate
authentic
threads
heresy
controls
white hunters
alcohol
abuse
custody
motivating
sit-down
leaders
nominated
by
mining companies
pastoral leases
progressive
impacts
and sustain
extinguishment!
as assistance
modifies acts
presence
traces
the local
and maintains
representatives

authentic
claims
to constitutional
strategy
faith
and ownership
rifles
revisionist
histories: lights
in the sky
shackles

Visitant Eclogue

Farmer

Well, I said to the missus that something pretty odd
was happening out here, this being the third night
lights have appeared over the Needlings; and she
said stay clear Ben Rollins, stay clear, don't go
sticking your nose into something you don't understand.
And I said, well it's my place and if anything weird
is up I wanna know about it. And it's just starting
to dry off in these parts, and it's almost a fire risk.
The everlastings will be out soon and they'll dry
until they crinkle like cellophane in the hot
easterlies, and like a blowtorch they'd go up
taking the surrounding paddocks with them.
So here I am, *touched by your presence*, not quite
sure what to make of it but knowing that this
is as big as it gets, that death'll have nothing on it.

Visitant

radiant inner heart countertracking epicycloidal
windrows and approaching harvest, as if to probe your body
like a contagion that'll never let you go,
corporate body politic, engraving crops
and stooking heretics, this our usufruct,
wickerman serving up the meek & generic
as vegetation names itself and the corpse
fills with a late shower, nomadic

emergent anticipation, toxic cloud of otherness
presence before authentic essay in defence
of time's minor fluctuations,
and we comprehend your gender,
missus as signifier to your gravelled utterance

Farmer

Now keep my missus out of it, she doesn't want
a bar of it — I've already made this clear. Hereabouts
it's mainly grain, though those offerings dotting the fields
in this brooding light are sheep that'll work in trails
down to the dam and struggle for shade or shelter beneath
a single tree. Around here used to be stands of mallee
and York gum, though I'm not sure what the natives
used to call it. Yep, they were here before us,
though there's none around now so I can't help you there.

Visitant

in family structure, as dialect wears out
and you claim ownership — down from the ship
we name and conquer, that's what you'd have us think,
to go your way and validate; scarifiers and hayrakes,
all aftermath and seed drilled to be ellipsed by grains
of superphosphate, expressionist and minimal
all at once, expanding tongues as if a place of worship
might spontaneously erupt, the face of a prophet
frowning in local stone, or grinning out of a piece
of imported fruit — the simplest is most exotic

Farmer

We've always been churchgoers, and I'm proud to say
that I'm an alderman; we've just got new bells
and they ring out through the valley like they're
of another world, and believe it or not, the congregation
has almost doubled in the last few weeks. I say
it's the bells but my wife reckons it's in the air,
that people feel depleted and need something
to absorb the emptiness. When pushed, she can't put
a finger on it. The minister has mentioned it in his sermons.

Figures in a Paddock

In their wake the furrows,
partings in long grass,
burrs hell-darning their socks
like recovered memories.

Parallel to the fence — star pickets
mark depth, interlock mesh
letting the light and visuals
through, keeping the stock

in or out — like religious tolerance.
Down from the top-road to the creek,
arms akimbo, driven against
insect-noise, a breeze that should

be rustling up a performance.
Towards the dry bed, marked
by twists and shadow-skewed
rivergums, bark-texture

runs to colour like bad blood.
The sky is brittle blue,
foliage thin but determined:
colour indefinable beyond green.

They walk, and walking makes history.
And tracks. All machinery.
The paddock inclines. A ritual of gradients.
Ceremony. Massacre. Survey.

Charlie

Getting his mouth around the vowels
in 'hello Charlie', cosmetically challenging
the Indian Hill mynah bird's four vocal
resonances, testing himself outside the grip
of its cage, white feathers still glistening
in the shade beneath the verandah,
sunflower seeds husked and scattered,
head bobbing and busy on the human spectrograph:
hello Charlie hello Charlie how's it going mate
how's it going mate . . . in a stream
that might almost be poetry; parchment tongue
chewing over the words, its beak a flesh gouger.
Object in its setting: a flutter of wings,
a child with a stick amusing itself
as the sulphur-crested cockatoo peels
the bark off in strips, fencing the sharpened foil,
taking each electric jolt. Cruelty
and excitement entangle themselves
and a new generation instantly understands
the craft of encagement. The backyard zoo
is how you're allowed to love animals.
It's the visitors who poke the sticks
when you're not looking, you tell yourself.
Charlie prefers old people and hangs
around with them for years. They share a cage.
They understand each other and talk incessantly.
Start stop. Vocal-cord. Frictional. Cavity modulation.

Syrinx. Trachea. Larynx. Tympaniform membranes.
Semi-lunar membranes. Simultaneous
production of notes. Talking to a bird.
To themselves. A neighbour or relative
drops by. They keep in touch.
The retirement years are the busiest.
They tell you. You tell yourself and Charlie
ages another decade. Going on fifty now.
Hello Charlie hello Charlie. A visitor
loses a fingertip. *Dance cocky dance cocky
dance cocky do*. You can't recall
why they cover his cage at night.

Anonymous

The Work Which Established Hirst's Reputation In The British Art World Is Entitled *The Physical Impossibility of Death in the Mind of Someone Living* (Pl.324), It Consists Of A Dead Tiger Shark Floating In A Tank Of Preservative Fluid. The Shark Has Been Balanced And Weighted So That It Floats In The Middle Of Its Tank, Just As Though It Were Floating In Its Natural Element. (*Artoday*, Edward Lucie-Smith, Phaidon, 1995) *or* The Use of The Word 'Its'

Its tank is as
an emerald and chilled sea,
drenched in protean light,
its gut filled with the leaden boots
of a lost solo circumnavigator,
tropical conjuring
of the Other,
in this Albion, this island state
as rare as uniqueness
or that *perfect* steak,
that attracted language-wise
and even geographically
Joseph Conrad,
and islanders such as myself
who know that sharks
can't afford to miss a beat —
drowning a threat to the machine that drives
their jaws, like art

and patronage
and representation: not the life-mechanism
but the weighting of a non-expanding universe;
hey, Damien, maybe
you've backed the wrong shark?
'It' the elemental nature, O
composited artist
of the dead, as if it belongs
to its own patch of turf,
the flesh advertised
(Saatchi Collection)
like a tiger consuming villagers
and being shot
out of 'necessity', its skin
elemental in its stately spread,
trophy with unique
life-giving properties,
a comfort to the living,
O *enfant terrible*,
provocateur,
bête noire
ad infinitum, fluid

Hockney's *Doll Boy* at the Local Country Women's Association Annual Musical: Wheatbelt, Western Australia

Opening night. As the curtain lifts
Doll Boy hovers in the wings,
the Town Hall full as the star drifts

centre-stage and in a falsetto sings
to the roar of the crowd —
the CWA already counting the takings

as the chorus of footy stars makes a loud
entry — smeared make-up and wigs,
ill-fitting blouses, the odd shroud-

length dress. A farmer digs
a mate in the ribs — that strapping
girl's my son, the last vestiges

of his reserve dissipating
with the electricity of the occasion.
At interval, the cast is buzzing

with excitement, taking slices of melon
from Doll Boy's chipped green plate,
blowing him kisses, calling him 'Queen'.

You're just not cute enough to rate
a place among us! Doll Boy, eyes
to himself, begins to create

a space apart, beyond the cries
of the crowd, the taste of melon on his lips:
sweet pink crystals bristling like stars,

full and sweet. And he grips
the memory of the vine — intricately
binding the patch near the roses and strips

of everlastings, ripening rapidly,
drinking the dam's muddy water insatiably,
preparing to feed the elect, delicately.

The Hierarchy of Sheep — a report
from my brother

1. Rams

To be lamb meat or castrated to wethers
or reign in longevity and fertility
and throw the shearer who can't afford
to hit back, golden balls hanging like trophies,
deep wrinkles genetically engineered
bringing the long merino wool as fine
as the buyer could want, as lambs
of an old ram with a kick so hard
that it takes a couple of roustabouts
to hold it down, will be as boisterous
and determined to take the world on —
'there is a lot of genetics in sheep,
even their temperament'.

A ram horns its way into the blue singlet
of a shearer and through to his belly,
coiled like the spiral matrix of hatred
recognising captivity — fly strike
thickening wool with goo and maggots,
possibly a rogue that's broken down fences,
furious amongst the ewes, savage to its fellows,
headbutting and cracking the competition —
the shearer wastes his enemy with a jet
of Aerostart up the nostrils, abusing the farmer

for feeding the bastard lupins and lime
while he watches on nervously, fearing a vengeful shearer
as the feelers sense their way out of the sheath
of the ram's penis — cut by the handpiece
the ram is rendered 'useless',
unable to find the ewe's cunt.

2. Ewes

All cut by a shearer at one time or another —
sewn together with dental floss or wearing their scars
gracefully beneath the new season's haute-couture,
role play as if gender has meaning out there —
collectively warding a fox from the lambs.
Earlier the farmer assisted a birth
and then shot a mother polluted by stillbirth —
utilitarian in the way of things. Months back
he'd joked as rams were unleashed
into a ripe flock; up with the crack of dawn,
watching the weather, noticing the comings
and goings of birds. Now rain threatens
and older ewes kick like hell,
all of them full with young, milk veins
up and pumping hard to udders —
somewhere a nick with a blade has a vein
knotted off with needle and thread,
the myth declaring that another takes its place.
'Sometimes ewes get nervous and sensing
their humility is not hard. They get this manic shake
and tears fall from the corners of their eyes.'

A lamb drops in a catching pen.
A shearer aims a teat at his mate
and squirts a shot of milk into his ear.
The shed is full of swearing and laughter.

3. Wethers

Low-maintenance power houses
scouring the goldfields for scant feed
their wool full of wool spiders, chewing
a shearer's singlet to extract salt
as the handpiece worms off a strip of flesh
and bleats come from somewhere deep
inside, wiry and up against it the farmer
keeping them on a slender thread
to boost the quality of wool — harsh
conditions producing fine strands.
A fly-struck wether with flesh
hanging in sheets and flies erupting
from its ribcage has a pesticide
sprayed into its cavities —
but not even this and the remnants
of testosterone can keep it upright
and a short while later the dull thud
of a gun being fired somewhere outside
moves contrapuntally into the shed,
teasing the buzz of the plant, downtubes whirring,
handpieces snatched in and out of gear.
Even the dead added to the tally.

4. Lambs

The assault comes on strong: tailed,
castrated, ringed, earmarked, and mulesed.
Tails gas-axed off. Alive and highly strung
and either moving on to weaner
then hogget then ram, ewe, or wether,
or consumed while the flesh is tender.

Drugs and Country Towns

for Paul Muldoon

The SS Commodore with tinted windows
will make the run to Perth in a few hours,

the stereo flat-tack and the driver pumped up,
hanging out but intoxicated by the prospect

of picking up, hollowness filled with bravado:
the deal better not fuck up or heads will roll.

A week's wages and a bunch of mates
who've put cash up front — the whole town

speeding off its face and strung out,
they'll be counting the hours

and tempers will flare, blokes
knocking girlfriends about,

bongs strained and beer on beer drained
to help them get through. The town is growing —

spreading out — out there ploughing,
listening to the call of the tawny frogmouth,

and then a run through the fast-food outlet.
Later, it's a mate's place for speed and videos.

Not yet big enough to hide rip-offs
those with contacts are jacking up the profits —

pharmacists, forcing frowns back
as they sell fit-packs and dieting tablets,

are asked to fill city prescriptions.
The older blokes are mumbling

at The Club — 'one of them young blokes
shore two hundred the other day

and the next day couldn't finish a run . . .'
The cops are getting rough — stripping cars

and raiding farm houses. They
have their chosen ones — boys

on the footy team, girls who do favours.
The world grows small fast — the town

moves out to the farms. Drive-ins
have shut down and fast music

comes into Country Hour
like Armageddon. On a back verandah

a farmhand says to his girlfriend:
'I love you . . . the sunset is magic.'

Funeral Oration

for Joyce Heywood

The grave is a gate you send flowers through,
and the pink blossom frosting the northern hemisphere
is, on closer observation, a confluence of species.
There is a scent that's as much about lingering
as leaving, and it's about time the ploughs
were moving down there. The geographical
centre fluctuates while the magnetic centre
remains rock solid. Prayer goes somewhere
and is not lost and expects nothing back.
An old tree — a York gum — oozes sap
like it's something special in this genealogy.
Most of the family is there and words are said
and those who can't attend wait for news of the dead
                as now it is all about memory.

Il faut cultiver notre jardin

Cleared land is a place of weeds,
bee-wings' razored whirr
and a cut trunk hollowed
by white ants — a font
beneath swabs of cloud.

When sunlight cordons
off an area for display,
hill-clefts and ravines
resist, retaining shadow.
Small birds sing and you

don't think of their name,
the air-drag of crows' wings
just overhead. Jam
trees keep their sap
tight beneath the bark.

Late winter warmth
dries cushions of moss,
rapidly brittle and crumbling
around purple sprays
of Paterson's Curse;

onion grass cuts low weather
and twenty-eights are caught
in a pause, a cessation
of dialogue — instruments
poised about the developing fruits

of the creek canopy.
Working their tails, chests
puffed and springing angles
like hearts, claws hooked
as numbers in a code

that won't quite scan:
but neither does God!
A globe-bodied spider
concentrates a poison
that bothers only flies,

mosquitoes and ants;
the sun intensifies and parrots
are burnt to silhouettes,
a clear night with frost threatens,
plants folding like prayer.

Hectic Red

Quartz sparks randomly
on the pink and white crust
of the salt flats, spread out
beyond the landing,
where bags of grain —
wheat and oats
in plastic and hessian —
lips sewn shut,
packed tight, flexing dust
and dragging their feet
to the edge, are tipped
onto the truck — feed-
grain, filling out
the flat-top, another body sack
waiting to be fed,
from top to bottom,
the sheep hollow-gutted
in the long dry, green-feed
deficient and this
the diminishing stock
of back-up tucker;
the best paddocks
up beyond the salt
all hoofed and bitten,
stray tufts targeted
and levelled,
dry roots crumbling

and dropping to dried-out
stream-beds beneath,
so no new encrustations
of salt emerge back down
in the low places, just the old crust,
pinking off — at night,
the crazy pick-ups
spinning wheels
and throwing headlights,
the bonnets rising and falling
in choppy waves, the light
as unstable as a camera
and the darkness dropping in
like black sacking; bleak rabbits
dashing about,
their blood infra,
the forecast — hectic red.

Gone to Seed

They'd convince you the weather
is fine — particles of sun declare
warmth, dryness, and sanity:
> *timor mortis conturbat me*

Seed companies deploy test
crops on soil neatly top-dressed,
rape, RED tomatoes, and soy
> *timor mortis conturbat me*

The terminator gene's rich
utility, deep sea fish
genes as anti-freeze — shiny:
> *timor mortis conturbat me*

Tilted on the x-ray machine,
the floors and walls polished clean —
interphased technology:
> *timor mortis conturbat me*

It's the welcome every trust
heaps upon the patient — lust
for health and equality:
> *timor mortis conturbat me*

Copywritten DNA
fragments, and begins to stray —
the structured fields look happy:
        timor mortis conturbat me

The West on the verge of conquest
stores patents in its war-chest —
the harvest feeds an army:
        timor mortis conturbat me

Obituary

for Yehudi Menuhin

A survivor of Belsen knows Menuhin
who was there with Benjamin Britten
a few weeks after liberation, delicately stirring
the spirit back to health. With temperatures rising
I find this poem almost complete as it is a piece
I would have written were he still alive. The choice
to sit among the plants with their breath of pollen
is something he'd have defended, the fallen
not forgotten but given new life, resonant
and stimulating growth. Despondent,
I have lost myself to sonatas and found
new points of reference: the sounds
of bird song, traffic in the distance,
the violin tender when most intense.

Sine qua non

Those apples I've struggled to write
for years — lines about cooking
and fermentation and decoration:
haphazard globes denting as they crash
to the path, tepid in the first days
of autumn, enjambed like invocation —
of days apart, polished by humidity.
The collapsing moment: the thrill
of encounter, the sticky fluid
of memory spread like a blemish.
Those stray trees untended
glower like wild planetariums:
a pleasure I'd neglect, brought
so close to you, here in the past.

Lyrical Unification in Gambier

for Marjorie

(i)

What remains barely the weather
report: sentencing labours of history
against all beginnings, the maples
leafless, the houses barely porous.

(ii)

I ride roads I am not familiar with,
a figure of speech, chrome strips
between windows. To the south,
burial mounds. Resolution
deep and simpatico. Northwards:
the lake effect, the snow plough.

(iii)

Deer go down to bow and gun,
roadkill is a 'cull': beauty
in the eye of rhetoric
keeps the engine
ticking over.

(iv)

Cornstalks like rotted Ceres'
thin black teeth. To end with this.
A season of political arrangements,
remnant snow quarried
like that pitiless ocean.

(v)

The driver must resist
all beauty, the smell
of an unfamiliar passenger.
A door rattles, the car
is almost new. It is shut
properly. Speed limit.
Farm machinery. A (solitary)
white field enclosed
by thawed pages.

(vi)

Maples, oak . . . all kinds.
A tornado ripped through here
three months ago and didn't
touch the houses either side.
Birds warble in the engine
cavity. A cord of wood
stretches out below
the kitchen window.
He says we listen
differently.

Poltergeist House Eclogue

Woman

You wait until we're alone in the house;
unsettling, destabilising, contra-indicating,
as if all should be calm here, not said
nor implied, the hum of the heating,
thermostat quavering, as if to prelude,
forewarn, distort a family photo.
This relationship is threadbare,
hanging on by a thread at best.

Poltergeist

Upset is not random, carefully planned
strategy, tactics are honed.
Council, community, mutual
understanding. Between us, a pact.
I move, we move, they move, only
where you want us to. Expectation,
tenterhooks, the book crashes to the floor —
you're on the other side of the table.
A seismograph registers, recording
at interstices of the body.

Woman

Investigate, don't run at first
provocation, imagine chance and external
occurrences, imagine distress
coming to a head: time-loss, faith
diminishing. A bird flew into the house
and dashed itself against the windows.
The light sharp outside, though frost
on the ground. I let it out. And still
books fell. And fall. We listen.

Poltergeist

Energy is data, first lesson we learn.
It has its own propaganda. Sexfeed,
screaming matches, making up . . .
things not bargained for. It's like
a package holiday. Like a shift
in the television schedule: she
searches hard beyond the image,
in there, amongst circuitry.

Woman

Small things falling, moving, almost
acceptable. But faucets all on or the carpets
changing colour anger me.
The threat of exorcism is tense in the house.
The worse it gets the less I mention
these goings-on. Just store it up,
verging on critical. The radio comes on.

Poltergeist

Leaving a situation is both hard
and comforting. You know someone
as much as you ever will if it's
that far gone. And you can't take
them with you, you go out alone.
As scripts and formula are written
and spoken, I turn the wine to water.
I send cracks through plaster.
I turn stomachs. We are gone.

The Burning of the Hay Stacks

'Laved in the flame as in a Sacrament . . .'
                                    – Thomas Merton

There was a rash of burnings
that autumn — the arson squad
said circumstances were suspicious,
but there was a lack of evidence
to pursue a prosecution.

Always at evening, in heavy weather,
humidity insisting something happen.
Storms came later, but there was no lightning
to blame. And the pattern pushed
the odds out of orbit: with a bit

of imagination, you could make five
points with the town as the centre.
Pentacle, Pentecost, pent-up energy.
The wick lit, they just erupted,
traces of sap crackling like trees

rundown by bushfire. At a point
above the stacks a blue halo, wavering
circle that looped down over the last light
of days just not right for seeding.
On the fifth occasion, the owners

of one property called on the Anglican
minister to do a blessing, and then, for good
measure, the Catholic priest. An old aunt
suggested looking back into the Old
Testament, talking persistently

about Jerusalem belonging to all religions,
of plagues and desert and exile,
her long-dead husband's Jewish roots
lost to the fires, the hidden fuel
that feeds the burning of hay stacks.

Chainsaw

The seared flesh of wood, cut
to a polish, deceives: the rip and tear
of the chain, its rapid cycling
a covering up of raw savagery.
It is not just machine. In the blur
of its action, in its guttural roar,
it hides the malice of organics.
Cybernetic, empirical, absolutist.
The separation of Church and State,
conspiracies against the environmental
lobby, enforcement of fear, are at the core
of its modus operandi. The cut of softwood
is deceptive, hardwood dramatic: just
before dark on a chill evening
the sparks rain out — dirty wood,
hollowed by termites, their digested
sand deposits, capillaried highways
imploded: the chainsaw effect.
It is not subtle. It is not ambient.
It is trans nothing. A clogged airfilter
has it sucking up more juice —
it gargles, floods, chokes
into silence. Sawdust dresses boots,
jeans, the field. Gradually
the paddock is cleared, the wood
stacked in cords along the lounge-room wall.
A darkness kicks back and the cutout

bar jerks into place, a distant chainsaw
dissipates. Further on, some seconds later,
another does the same. They follow
the onset of darkness, a relay of severing,
a ragged harmonics stretching back
to its beginning — gung-ho,
blazon, overconfident. Hubristic
to the final cut, last drop of fuel.

Polytype

'A school of fish, not accepting the inclusion of water
In concept . . .'
— Che Qianzi (trans. Jeffrey Twitchell)

They moved in the evolving countenance
like a street demonstration, missing in action
the blooming reportage, wave crests & troughs
      enforcing chapels on the fringes
      of tidy towns, the waterways
heavy-weeded and red-bloom algae succulent,
an indifferent ode to otherness, this whimsical
criticism of cells, obtunding this Matthew Arnold.

A right idea has no history, just punches
in the old time clock decorating the tessitura.
They heard him sing when IT was at its finest.
      Job security. A Titian. *The Gypsy*
      Madonna a fusion of non sequiturs
and false names. Low otherness of systems
they see and follow politely, dispersing memoria.
Too late on Etna Empedocles this gory discipline.

Technology is not in language. Murmured soliloquy.
Calque and gnosis: they saw you there leaning
casual against the mob, unloading your Nikon
      which subverts the throw-aways.

Unless the plant is soulless. Un-
admit the feeling. In spite, the nourishing
as by word of mouth the sea grows sticky. Drinking
incomplete, as feeder & decay implicate the proper food.

As policy the open door contempts the verbal. The askance
of kingdoms lotused up & sold as image. They are
different there. There, they are, as they should be.
        In translation. Poise, the deep dry
        river bed can't stand the season, & the changes
come too slowly. Prose-lapse the pilgrimage. As fish eggs
blow like sand against the banks they walk in sequence.
Credit a potential phonogène; let's enjoy the silence.

Mirror script a practical science, in seventh heaven
they dropped a letter of base utterance, u ho, ho hu in the
crowded jokes, as if a linguist should drink too much,
        glossing ethnographies and writing-up as
        should be read. Oral emulations take essay
with deliverance as warping chases the quoinish furniture.
The point is to redeem the text as glory & joy. Finesse
the bordered register. Precise a slight hilarious dish.

Every Now & Again Thoughts of Bombay
Enter the Heads of Those in Bangalore

pre-dawn road-sulking in the garden city
some strolling or waking up or perishing in Cubbon Park —
why go elsewhere(?) — Chaturvedi Badrinath
of *The Times* [printed in Bombay] says the foundation
of human freedom & night in Dharma & Jainism
are radically different from those
that are provided in the western political
& legal philosophy of modern times.>this place
is pure(ly) structure's lists of the unbuilt & un-
finished like languages evolving
with social predicaments so new stories are added
well & truly lived in
satellite dishes like cribs of images
beggar bowls aimed to heaven —
becoming clearer
they neglect groundswell(s)
of opportunity (in Bombay
the stock-exchange is thriving!)
as Ta Ta trucks ARE their own trend
passing luminescent (but) smog-washed[?] BUT glowing
boulevards of optimism, the script
as clichéd as eucalypts
around Bangalore University — fluoro tubes
& whitewash & Hamlet prowling
or maybe skulking in the heat, dark eagles
shadowed Möbius against the skyline

while below, stealth moves with dogs, pigeons, parrots,
sparrows, rats & a white-tipped wingéd creature
that circle images of Ganesh, olfactory & sensing
every crow-movement, scent[ed] offering of orange
white & yellow flowers
piled high & illuminating all roadside temples
betwixt neo-Dravidian state legislature
discouraging beggars but not tourists
who take more & unwittingly drink tap water
from branded bottles

What with the mass exodus of
models to the land of milk and
money, local choreographers weep
with frustration at the thought of
their carefully nurtured beauties
only working with the likes of
Hemant Trivedi and Lubna Adams.
Well, given the general standard of
the local-yokels, who'd want to work
here anyway? Especially when you
think of the pittances the poor
models get paid, compared to what
they earn in Bombay. Well, the
choreographers only have themsel-
ves to blame, for in their desperation
to get work, they quote the most

[202]

ridiculous of rates to their local-
yokel clients and then force the local
models to perform in abysmal
shows a staff reporter for
Bangalore This Fortnight writes
with a fit of pique

warnings over handling
corpses which may harbour
disease appear as lit. theory
on the walls of bookshops
while crickets chirrup so loud
the trees hum like circulars in the state
library in Kidney City as organs
are quickly put on ice for transfer
into richer bodies but this
is poverty just like splendid saris
near the aquarium which promotes
fish as brain food
& the first jet made in India
shooting frozen flames on a muggy day
as somebody reads that <in his messianic drive
against eunuchs, pimps, brothels and gambling dens,
Mr Navalkar would often don garbs & disguises,
even wearing an afro wig on one occasion to gather
information on Bombay's sexual habits> while
nearby Vidhana Soudha in neo-Dravidian
[state secretarial & legislature], unlocks a cabinet door
of pure sandalwood, carves art as policy
& repeats the Pandora's box of campaign victories —

at least in the memories of the seasoned legislators,
& Attara Kacheri with new Corinth-ian-
esque columns poured in concrete &
Visvesvaraya Industrial & Technological
museum & Venkatappa Art Gallery &
glam houses & crystal palaces & Parsi Fire Temple
& Ganapati Temple & Sampangi Rama Temple
& St Marks & St Marys are noted by
the traveller in the all-day-hire taxi
moving through Bangalore like the slow evacuation
of congestion while at the Dravidian
bull temple by Kempe Gowda, the
bull wandering & consuming all groundnuts
despite resistance appeased only by the temple
& a celebration
of the victory of ART like divining
& astrology (it reveals, Tantra relieves) & predicting earthquakes
& the Nehru Planetarium
& the green waters of Ulsoor Lake
& the Maharaji's imitation Windsor Castle
& banyan trees, neem & flame trees, shikakai tree
that ground down keeps the hair clean
like the mynah bird knowing who it was
that killed Laura Palmer
while Kempe Gowda 1 made Ulsoor
to store drinking water for his troops

& Dom Moraes reads between the tenses
in Bombay: 'The lonely traveller is warned
                    That ours is not a safe territory
                    Since Rictus from the cave returned'

Across the road from the hotel a line is forming outside the gates
of the Galaxy Cinema. The billboard glowers Hum Aapke Hain
Koun! A man & a woman. The man in braces & a white linen shirt
leans out of the frame & looks determinedly up to my fourth floor
window. He knows me. The woman leers at him. The line of
cinema goers recognise the conniving wife in her. This is a film
about power. Her sari is orange & silk & suggests Bombay liberalism. The
                    bamboo
scaffolding (festooned?) with crows is about to collapse. It is an old
cinema. Eagles circling overhead are zinc-grey, dust brown
& as money changes hands
there is closure.

Ornithology

They set out before dawn with optical instruments
pens and notebook. By the lake they will create
poems without reference. This refuge in the suburbs
covered in mist like a smokescreen, the traffic nearby

moving to and from another front. Night herons
will be making their way to daytime roosts
while vast flocks of cormorants and ibises
will be shaking the droplets of night moisture

from their wings. Ripple-flex will break the lake
with the first dives of a darter, serpent high-headed
on a technical neck. The sun's appearance will subvert
the abject waters. [Rhythm is shock as all erupts.]

(ii)

One observer whispers *cacophony*, the others say
don't interrupt. It cannot be determined who joins in on
this riposte, so none can be quoted. The birds are prosy
one might suggest but translation is tyranny —

traduire, c'est trahir, referring to crib notes as per habit
and (migratory tendency). An odd bird lifts blithely and they
simultaneously gesture, forgetting birds or explanations
or flight. *This bird developed of itself in isolation?*

the Russian ornithologist asks. *Its call is beyond our own*,
his Australian hosts reply. He seems satisfied and takes note.
Under the heading 'Ostranenie' he writes: a night
heron awakening with sunrise, and going about its

swamp-stalking business in full light, weight of the old world
on its shoulders, threatening closure, drip-dry feathers
coming unstuck and tilting disdainfully contrary, rejecting
camouflage in the roots of swamp paperbarks, denying

its geography, blurring genre. That this should happen diurnally
does not spoil the observation. These binoculars being *trained
to look where they shouldn't* in this upside-down climate.

Frame(d)

for Karl Wiebke

erosion mimics a frame
like the severed limb retained:
raison d'être a vacant twitch
of the lip, placed in such
& such a non-littoral, but
inner like litotes cut out
of bridgehead & speech & speculative
shoulds that lie beneath

water: praising all THAT
fraught like ambiguity,
yeah, just a series of cross-
hatching, tide & tesserae
gauges of temperature: flow-
set in solid shadows or float-
ed against the picaresque
as distance

otiose, no neat slabs
defining banks of algae
red as graffiti, the
ordinance of iron & water &
yes, over, over the bridge

interplay: they careen hulls
rotten of colour &
greedy for detail: light-
ships & deadbanked &
dead-eyed as they scrape non-
quant
itative modes of seeing, or shrouds
of dead
feyes in the topsailed
balusters, we lean against the rail

where is it we see
this vast field of outers

                                                                                                                           &

&

ravishing inners, smoothly
ravishing inners, smoothly
prized apart as text — UR
&

enjambent over & under
& only in disbelief
does the hardened bream

fisher accept his hollows
came with bridge & dredge
& steep vertical in-deep
but needing obviously to outdrift the damage
in defining or redefining or holding to task
the engineer did not think to glance beneath
                    the gloss

we see from betwixt & hear AND, a visual mix like planes
as aerodones, refuse & list in curves the waves' trans-
lations as taken meanings, & we must taste the acrid frame,
but re-
                    fuse to be drawn entirely

                    THE as seals are scuppered, so so small
the tiny coda that eats the larger rotting fish:
                    as embroidery to cerulean depth
& tableaux of scrutiny

Calendar: A <u>Continuous</u> Narrative

'Just look around . . . you'll see wonders'

June

Our year starts here, a dank
wet South, dust dry
North. In between, there's
nothing definitive. But being
an inflection of *your* climate
we'll remain as far under
as possible.

July

The trees here that are bare
are European with few exceptions.
The widow maker sits glumly
though retains its foliage.
In summer it absorbs moisture
and drops limbs [<u>indifferently</u>]
now only cold winds cut
its mordant flesh.

August

diagnostically the limitations
of winter strain the capacity
of the power grid, storms
lacerate the Unions
and Jim is hot-under-the-collar
outside Parliament.

September

The 'boat people'
are still incarcerated
in the Port Hedland
Detention Centre,
Land Rights Claims
are choking the courts
into inactivity,
the mining companies
are doing deals
on the side,
the oil brews
in the Timor Gap.
Amongst the peonies
and daisies blue leschenaultia
is blooming.

October

Carpets of everlastings
are lifted from the scrub
and relaid in city mansions.

November

They're harvesting in some places now,
at least in the central wheatbelt,
deeper south the crops are still green
and it will be Christmas to the New Year
they're working. The calendar
being particular to location,
like the markings on seed packets,
the stimulants to growth.

December

Cyclone Frank is off the West Coast
and cyclone Emma is hitting Christmas Island.
That's North, but the fallout reaches you here
eventually. Sullen weather,
that threatens to jam
two climatic zones
together. On either side
of the degenerative low
it's stinking hot.

January

Month of the Republic.
The beaches full
and lashings of zinc cream
staining the sea.
The sun so harsh you dare not expose
your skin on clear days between
ten and three, or if you're into denial,
saying it *can't happen to me*,
between eleven and two.
A national bronzing,
a cargo cult in melanomas.

February

Sometimes on a sultry evening
the harsh dry compresses
into a sudden rush of perspiration,
thunderheads

build over the river and break
with a flurry of lightning,
the shattered luminescence
of obscured, swallowed sun.

Cameras on the foreshores attempt
to capture the definitive etching,
pyrographic over the purple
skies like indelible pencil.

The wetlands scorched and irritable,
deep below the watertable wallows,
the bush firebrigades on the city's outskirts
on high alert, sinking heaps of beer.

March

Congestion stalks the initial
windfalls like haiku full-blown
with humidity but then with a sudden
rush of heat struck dumb, desiccated,
wizened under the insistent sun.

April

A sultry month, but the nights
are often chill. There is little balance
between outside and inside atmospheres.

May

A May election is not technically possible
but the mood if it were would be unforgiving,
driven against the zones of comfort
in the hardenings of the coming winter.
A referendum can be terminal
but it's pretty mild here comparatively,
they call it *Mediterranean*,
in this Yued place, matrilineal moieties,
patrilineal descents grouped locally, Nyungars
incarcerated for stealing the not so golden fleece.

The Rust Eclogues: Radnóti, Poetry, and The Strains of Appropriation

(i) autoecious

the appropriation of a host
in the random dispersal
of words, hard investments
in the soft tissue
of national identity,
the singular mind is the passion
of heritage, the aspect of blood,
the notion hosting
the struggle, the call up
of the one body on which the soul
is parasite enough, as if there's
a need to talk with the words
you live off, their buzzing growth,
their singular obsession
with death as seasonally
significant
in this and more, as if you
couldn't say this is THE
auto da fé, as if accrued
love would be filed, 'I' with this single
species shall examine need,
and as the host grows wizened
the spores make as if airborne
delivering yesterday's news

you are only living
through the communications
with a self that offloads
a myriad of voices
into autopilot, collecting
black box data
obsessively,
that internally
the dark cell
can't disappoint,
like dialogue
between soul and self
and the conceits
of biotechnology,
as if safe from an informing
segmented space,
as if no one looks in
on solitary, as all
surveyed remonstrate
with the instant view
of the multitudes: spores
anatomical, political,
well disciplined.

(ii) heteroecious

Riven in the folds and clefts
like envy
it increasingly absorbs light

and wallows on moist days
harbouring tetanus
and rendering food crops
and collections of Hungarian
postage stamps
worthless, all hosts mutable
and fair game; its refrain
is soundless
and yet it reverberates
through all industry,
keeping the bastards honest
or sending them broke,
incorporating the oxidation
of nutrition and wealth, the symbols
of growth edging out the lustrous crop
as a fantastic collusion
of season and labour,
the lyrical eyes standing
linear and outside,
itself, no longer reliable
in the newly-made contexts,
become the compound adjective
in its manipulation
from past participle, like the gender
indiscretions of bread-making
from the very same nineteenth
century strain of wheat, maybe
from the fields of metaphor,
or cross-fertilized
in the language laboratory,
the leering investigative eyes
of the ag. department.

Sharecropping
as dross around the mouthpiece,
the seamy vigilante-ism of the press,
the glittering surfaces
defecting like layers
on layers of hate,
just being lesser degrees
of love in the conscription
of appropriate doctrines
to good feeling, the indulgences
they call appropriation,
the well feds of American
poetry, the wells where sound is absorbed
and yet rings in the water appear;
the reddish brown surface
discolouration
is the racism of words
as the weather hums
a few bars of a heritage
listing. Jealousy driving
the creative urge, poetry
the spiritualism of the material
religions. A few chips or flakes
in a test-tube, a glassine
envelope, the chart
in the sampler's hut,
the glamorous intrusions
of popular culture on old-ish
negatives, the consternations
of hyperspace outing random

associations of alliterative infestations,
the escape velocity, the mass of a star,
against poetry, which is like
an Elizabethan village showing
the old arts, no longer
cells watched over by
the commercially fetishised,
the contracted panopticon
is the lookout, and all is one,
and the profits roll if in the greater
stack the rust is diluted
and sold off before it can take hold,
consolidate, thicken, colonise,
procure, absorb, digest,
consume, render even the highest
quality product worthless. Ro-
tating the expansion
we contract the better half
like sharecropping,
documenting the 'common
identity', the self
of nationhood though some
of the we having cleaner hands
and bribing the sampler.
The stack is cleared
or dispersed beyond
the edges of the map, and that's that.
A new season, a stainless steel
multi-voiced and glamorous
factory. A spectacle!

Marginalia

'Smooth verse, inspired by no unlettered Muse . . .'
— 'The Excursion', William Wordsworth

Unlettered nature
pshaws the annotation
roused up and bordering
distinctly white torrents

A series of parallel
circuits lights up
in the boy's eyes

Scene from above,
the sands of
the hour glass

Textual reruns
whose crimes
flaw us;

Hah! Likely
story — existing
without quote marks,

Soft effects.

Breathers

for John Ashbery

The new world's breathers simulate an Attic vase —
hoplites red-lining against the public hum, kicking
        up their heels as shields almost overlapping
take the rap, a fashion show beneath the glow
of a hustling city vicarious as the weirs open & close,
open & close, as if the locks of some minor river
        meandering inland might offload its traffic,
counter sidereal the choking graphics of the charts,
        all higher than the pleasant banks of grass,
trinkets of community busy in adulterating arts,
graceful in robes of ancient sailcloth, the designer
insisting on simplicity and sweet neglect as below
        the crowds scramble to meet their
debts, their need for breath and the artist's trick

I unsubscribe

mis demean our refuse
topped sub due, a lawn
and stippled verb, test
ice-top, signifiosis
stranger in private proprietory
cased in language
replies unrequested,
requiet paced across
sharp grassblades,
hypo, and where locate
geno flex ion buddings,
where petit déclassé
testamental cultures,
columnular scroll, temples
and feathers parsed
odour, outré

Why Write No Poetry More

estfavour, pour gramrare
incur, askew, aka insistentor
saqueneme est fixator
in, preser vert er stockist
clust, awed upclaw
un apologia, lyris
instignation, foreclose
upythesis, gerd luca
placirds, erd air,
syrios

& Succor

inist geothemies sistic, treple upclass -ments,
axiomies, I sest readentary: drinkables, thirst sents

func gigs up crites, less lovely, encircled festeries
can as can do, fuck hit'n duelists says groups, treez

Rain Gauge

Millpoint throaty guzzler, wishful
choker as dust films throat, to measure up,
squalls with hooks and introversions, bale-hooks,
moebius comeback though sharp and sliced
from the same stretch, to hang up or catch skin
to ripen blood-eating earth, so sharp needles
of rain crosscut, score soil and tease seeds,
to calibrate the empty out and add up,
it says enough but penetration's not there
and lateral spread, its absorption
which is not a formula of depth, width, impact,
even with the resistance, the failure of soil
to wet, taken into consideration. What factor
has us check the gauge when the crops are in,
when growth is simply about moisture,
to engage the rainmaker, the seeder of air
when airseeders have percolated hectare
after hectare of earth, to balance the equation,
the anti-matter or parallel universe of planting
and growth, the balanced equation of faith
that adds up so each seed sprouting
spites and despites the rain gauge
as if miracles can blossom from the negative?
They can't, and even moisture from the sea
won't reconcile tropes and impositions,
and the miracle of rain we might not even see
will be seen in crops and wild grasses,

good foliage on even hardy resistant trees,
less salt in low damp spots — an adjustment
in contradictions, apparent laws
we apparently live by, bothering the gauge
after sleep's deliberations, blanks and deletions.

180 Degrees of Separation

The sheep came here before entering the yard
for the killing: he would cut their throats

with a short, worn knife. I have written
about this in a variety of ways. I keep

rewriting the same poem. But there were
many occasions I *witnessed* — the word's

appropriate — and a book entirely composed
of poems about sheep killing would not

be enough. Maybe a line for each organ?
A page for each carcass? A section for the skins

laid out over the fence — oily and yellow inside.
The wool shorn back to the uncoloured outer skin

month after month. Years. Decades.
He kept the freezer full of sheep parts.

I'm sure he didn't enjoy what he did — it was work.
He noted the pigs enjoyed the innards

dumped from the barrow. The cold brought
steam, the heat a stink that permeated.

An outdoor task — below the shed overhang —
for all weathers. The frightened bleat like a storm.

What I've not considered is the shape
of the paddock where the sheep selected for killing

waited out their time. Only a few, the feed
was rarely under pressure. A triangular paddock,

its angles went from relatively open to suffocation.
The sheep, I recollect, rarely grazed in the narrow

point — the angle furthest away from the killing yard
and slaughter hook. They moved on trails looped

across the broad end of the field, the end nearest the dirt
with its red inside red: like oil-stains that go a long way

below the surface, sit on the water table. Float.
I wonder if the shape of the paddock was coincidence

or convenience: the mathematics of bottlenecks
and imperative, the sides always adding up: the half-life,

the lifting out of the herd: there was no random
gesture in the killing, and the prejudice

was lost as good people grew used to it.
Forgive them Lord, they know not what they do?

Crop Duster

It is the noun behind the action
that wrecks the choral work,
stiff breeze across drought-tweaked
ears of wheat charged with late rains,
aerofoils catching and sweeping
aquatic, harmonic exhalations
of scrub and pathways
that survey undulations; for here
the crop duster, sharp single-seater
with gull wings displaying,
ballet parody, stench of poison
imposing the shadow of a suppressive
kiss: Cape tulip a legacy
on uncropped surface,
serial movements of emblematic parrots
escorting, switching at low-level
transfer stations, to bind the journey;
crop duster, aerial sprayer, farm-acology
mapped in the iris, as if seeing clouds
of spray billow out will necessarily
suggest a bitter odour, ingestion,
despite the wind blowing
in the opposite direction,
and we in our porous skins,
moving fast and further away.

Mowing

It's a rev thing this ingenu
contemplates as his bum vibrates
and ball-sack shakes, whipping
his sperm to a cream or frenzy,
or wiping out the last ones —
those missed by the herbicides
he dumps on the firebreaks.
It's hard to revel in winter greenery
chopped to a herby piquancy,
to feel a renewal come out of the red dirt
you know it disguises; strap-on, ride-on flirt,
he skirts fruit trees bare as the nudity
that takes him to the refrigerator
when the rest of the house sleeps,
his curvaceous paddocks close and smooth,
velvet on a flawed skin rising up
to meet him with every thrust.

A Swarm of Paragliders

Over the mountain they vacillate.
Not quite flies over dung — the mountain
is too good for that. And flies land —
these hover, and resist landing as long
as possible. They need the mountain
to stay up there — in their bullshit freedom,
coming down as far away from their launch place
as they can. Setting club records. Causing
distress to old men in fields and kids alone
in farmhouses when their cell phones
are out of range. I type looking up at them
over the mountain. Through camera lenses
they could see the detail of my scrunched face.
They are perverts, though consider
themselves without social boundaries
up there, above it all.
The drifts, lifts, drops, curves, and circlings
are sexual. They are frustrated. They are
of the same family as sky divers. When
I was in rehab almost a decade ago
one of the counsellors or nurses or doctors
or all of them suggested I go for a sky dive,
that its rush, its extremity, would satisfy
any craving that might be lurking
in the place where these things lurk.
I look up at these losers
and wonder if they've taken the bait: it's like that,

soul-fishing, killing the client, the victim:
up there, letting the air and a bird's eye
view wash over their frustrations,
their brightly coloured chutes full of the sub,
high, luminous, caught up in the mix of control
and where the breeze might take you:
a thermal deceit.

Rodeo

Ay-o-rodeo, hooray!
  Rodeo, rodeo, yay!
    Some say it will stay
    Even when they
Cart it far away, far away!

Wheel-less, it bogs down in clay,
  Leafy suspension dismay,
    Rust in the chassis
    Motor antsy,
The tray-top of the Rodeo

Is sieve-like, the Rodeo's
  tray-top is sieve-like. Hooray
    Ay-o-rodeo,
    Hey, rodeo!
A long way from the factory.

All about the enamelled
  Body, tufts of Cape tulip
    Lash and flurry, strip
    Economy
Those robots in the factory.

O rodeo, Rodeo,
  Rodeo, rodeo, O,
    Under crow gestalt,
    Not far from salt,
We praise your brand-name, your shattered

Windows; the silver trimmings
  Stripped to the name Rodeo,
    Mauvaise foi, as your
    Aerial claws
The smoky air, rodeo!

Once we whipped you up into
  A lather, a glint in your
    High beam, those burn-outs
    We used to tout
At crossroads, Rodeo, a show!

Ay-o-rodeo, hooray!
  Rodeo, rodeo, yay!
    Some say it will stay
    Even when they
Cart it far away, far away!

Map: Land Subjected to Inundation

So that's salt, *the* salt, wonderland wanderlust
comeuppance, coo-ee refractor, TV static-inducer,
sullen receptor when crystals dampen
and melt, form a suggestion, this land
on the York map, Avon District, South-west Land Division,
South-west Mineral Field, fed by stream intermittent,
as high winds are ossified into not-that-far-off
contours and cliffs, trigonometrical station
                                          on the infinitesimally
small reserve crowning Needlings Hill, which the now-'owners'
won't let us climb:
                    so how does that feel?
                                    Uncle Jack's
old homestead 'Avonside' is listed, a square peg in a round hole
transmuted by grid convergence against the sheet centre,
                                                interferon
fighting intrusion of recollection,
                            that road we cut-up
on the Kwaka 100, small cc'd trail-bike that was big to us
and raced '28' parrots in their lifts and dips
drawn out:
            they really *do* drag you off.
                                    Contour lines
show a gradual falling away — not that dramatic.
                                        Wallaby Hills
at 59.2300 ha is only a semi-reasonable patch
set aside

for the conservation of flora and fauna,

and we know
the fence is down on the Melbong Creek side and sheep
wander through into a place where their dead brethren are dumped,
grazing diminishing species of plants.

This isn't for the sake
of the sheep, but the farmer extending the realm of grazing
to bulk them out, add a dimension to the quality of wool.
The landloss, water-tones sourced in the telephone paddock,
house dam paddock, running down through salt
as a drawcard, like an osmotic filter, sheep skin
a catalyst to seepage, and salt clustering
all about —

it's the shape,

the string in solution,
wide-eyed and close to formations,

avatars and hucksters,
deeply serious holders of the 'Boyl-ya',

whom you respect
and fear:

in subjugating and making his *Vocabulary
of the Dialects of Southwestern Australia*, Captain Grey
noted of the Boyl-ya-gaduk, that flight and dispersal
in air are a pleasure, had at will, or a pleasure to transport
in such a fashion, as invisible they'll force entry as a shattering
of quartz and consume flesh,

these chips of white and apricot quartz
littering the waste of the place now labelled as 'land

subjected
to inundation', that we call The Salt.

[238]

                              This creek or system of creeks
came out of the homeplace, fed by any poisons applied
to enhance the crops, fuel the generator that pushed out
little over thirty volts,
                              creek system that fed and feeds Pitt Brook
that feeds the Mackie River that feeds the Avon, contributing
to the salinity of the valley, this salt mine, this source
vicariously 'ours',
                    left behind, enriching
the nation's coffers, comeuppance, a sullen receptor
where crystals dampen and melt.

Borrow Pit

for Andrew Duncan

To gnash the gravel, 'winning' they call it,
a pit just in from Mokine, down Waterfall — the roads
hereabouts, the gravel tops that slide like watersheds,
top-dressed with laterite efficacy, as where the bush is demolished,
twenty feet deep the clay and gravel are extracted,
now a dumping pit — household, property-making waste,
piles of dead trees and dead sheep, runnels
and washouts, this God in lines; at the rim
powderbarks, mallee, a centrifugal gulley,
parrot bush . . .
                bulldozed sub-edges,
                            radar dish, deflecting
messages back to the source — this being no place
for thermometers;
                so winning your winning ways,
so borrowed and charcoal of visited fires,
shadows that contradict a fireban, small birds
in cutting bushes,
                the '28s' almost *discrete*;
                            it imposes itself,
this discovery, more so for climbing up into the mallee,
more so for a stay shorter than we like;
                        what can be sourced
where a lingering wildlife owes it all to the roads

insisted, good state of repair, rarely used
and only by a few farmers and their families,
commodity,
                    the 'ute shooting thing', power trap,
horrified, those shadows. I position myself,
this gravel pit, the bark stripping
from flooded gums a few miles away
where on *warning* land the gravel falls,
runs thinly when dry is dead-set everywhere. Ennui
is this God I know though can't feel: willing
on pitted stone, looking molten
in bush about the pit, like meteorites
coagulated, decked out like a living museum — specky.
The body clock is a barometer, like veins that knit
with our partner's sleeping together, or alone, bind us to the bed,
stimuli from the dead.
                    The stark blue sky sucks primaries
from the pit — winning gravel. Its cadenza
shape gives the illusion of water or epithets.
It takes scree to collude where water
is past or a ruse — I search them out, these places
to fill in the space — an emptiness that clarifies
pluralities. They are like letters or signs of grammar —
even syntax in its entirety — scooped out. The sounds of parrots
and honey-eaters an antidote to language,
                                    an antidote
to borrowed visions. Shit, what of me? So far below
the thin surface, fertility . . . reseeding will bring trees
flourishing out of the gravel clay. They plant them, sometimes,
to fill in the gap. A reclamation that might

lead to reserve status, a nominal forbidding
that will still attract triple-twos, kids-on-weekends with twenty-twos
cracking hornet hollow points,
                              the chest-fuck twelve gauge:
they might even claim environmental
good husbandry, ridding the vicinity, the borrow pit,
of rabbits and foxes . . . and we know what too many roos
can do. Wankers.
                    In cast-offs we meditate, the midday glow
down through the branches of a powderbark chewing the gulley,
chemical in its winning way,
                              the unnameable odour
of its bark, the nameable odour of its leaves.
In this heat, it's not hard to taste a place
from a few days ago, a year ago, from childhood.
In middle lives the shadows dilute in paddocks,
cleared spaces, and gravel pits the tear-away places
ripped up by teenagers on Kwaka trailbikes:
                                        how much
of this penance acquires its vantage point, its skulduggery
of prayers, its wrestling with fence-post pivots, the plough
discs, the antipathy of trucks bogged to the axles
in sweat.
          I borrow those moments, those high notes
of anticipation the early morning galahs ripping about,
chucking fits by the low ground;
                              I borrow words
from before I could speak, the tones of wandoo and mallee,
intricacies of roots, and palettes of gravel
that stare us in the face, trunks horizontal, parallel
to the rippling undersurface, those winning ways.

[242]

Redneck Refutation

I didn't connect regardless
how much I participated, it's a vocab thing
though not to do with skills of expression;
                                      ejecting bullets
from the breech, freezing whole carcasses
of home-slaughtered sheep, the contradictions
roll the same roads, and families
still come to visit:
                        dope crops in the bush, sullen days
coming down off bad speed, scoring from the old bloke
shacked up with teenage girls,
                              his bull terrier
crunching chickens;
                    a flat in the city is a deal
that can go either way, and the economics
of the paddock are the call-girl's profit;
                              the Ford Fairmont
runs against the speed camera, and blind grass
poisons sheep — sightless like the minister
amongst his flock,
                  the school teacher,
                      the father
who won't let his son play netball because it will turn him,
like an innocent bitten by a vampire, into a pervert — or worse —
a poofter. Outside, you can't know that those of us
who speak in short, inverted sentences
always have fences in a state of disrepair,

                                        line length
and wire length are directly proportional,
eloquent subdivider of land, intensive pig farmer,
will let nothing in or out, though the space around the pig-shed
is large and open, mainly used for hay cutting
while all sons play Guns N' Roses' *Appetite for Destruction*,
timeless classic . . . apotheosis, serrated road edge
where a termite mound astoundingly remains intact: there
are no generics, no models of behaviour.
                                        It's not that my
name is a misnomer: it's *who* owns
a particular conversation.

The Damage Done

Someone is revving the shit out of a chainsaw;
We look up from flatlands to the wooded summit,
Up past the hillside paddocks, up at the place of law.

Policemen don't go there, it's not their law,
Whitegums cast no shade over sheep, roots of wattle vibrate,
Someone is revving the shit out of a chainsaw.

After the heatwave, vandals cut wood like straw,
The damage done out of sight, we hear them harvest into night,
Up past the hillside paddocks, up at the place of law.

Tomorrow, in extrovert morning light, it will be hard to ignore
Their lines of light, ghosts of the outcrop trapped in granite,
Someone is revving the shit out of a chainsaw.

Night birds stuck in raw, dark air, left to claw
Phantoms and microwaves, asides in the script,
Up past the hillside paddocks, up at the place of law.

Down here, the parrots have returned — there are more
Than we thought. They scan for seed out of habit.
Someone is revving the shit out of a chainsaw,
Up past the hillside paddocks, up at the place of law.

Salt Semi-Ode

Maligned but part of the place,
the city feeds on rural disgrace,
tendrils of learning reach out
into the wheatbelt, and devout

critics research remnant bushland
until seeds can no longer purchase sand,
and science becomes art as poets
build Sodom and Gomorrah, and visionary boats

sail out on halcyon mirages,
all colours played by crystals,
shimmering blankness and wire-rust gauges,
poverty and sadness as expansion stalls.

Among the Murk I Will Find Things to Worship

Among the murk I will find things to worship,
the memory dressed up in acrylics, dawn-
haze training scrub on the mountain, bird-exchange
        tossed up around them.

That probity will move independently
rocks the river red gum, roots set down below
the salt line, a monoplane grinding the air,
        droning tepid clouds.

Christ, down-wind, picks up the static, facing us —
offers least resistance; down in the city
we eat with the Buddhists, admire the Jewish
        critic in traffic.

Amid she-oaks the Prophet stirs the thornbill,
the galahs cut their jagged about-face flight,
rust and oily residue slick the river,
        and yet, deny them!

The old man has lost his farm, moved into town —
huddles in the kitchen, Metters stove burning
low, rubs the emblem from his tractor's bonnet,
        calling heaven down.

Before and After the Famine

Before and after the famine
my Irish family of mountain woodmen,
went south to the curios of southern lands,
to hack their bit of bravado
out of the forests and wetlands.

A foreigner here, it strikes me,
a hundred and sixty years ago
my great great great grandfather
might have found it cheaper
to cross the sea sideways.

That would make me an anarchist
with American citizenship,
and if they stripped it from me,
it'd still be my country as birthplace.
The tubed magazine of my father's

rifle would make pepperpots
of road signs that warn rockfall
or flooding, and Johnny Cash
would still play on the portable stereo
out by the vegetable garden
he *won't put in this year* but does.

My Father Has Never Been to America

My father has never been to America
but when I think America I think of him —
a life in Kenworth trucks, admiration
for the company reps flown down
to show them how to do it for Australia.

My father sticks with the government
because they're keeping things pretty much the same;
he thinks gridiron's a dickhead's game
and Bud is like drinking urine,
but otherwise it's America all the way.

My mother has been to America
and likes to speak other languages.
She recognises English is not the only way.
She constantly tries to vote out right-wing
governments, and though fearing the police,

thinks it's good the protestors
peacefully stand up to the evil empire.
She admires the politeness, not the policing.
My mother and father divorced
when I was seven — my mother
worshipped Elvis, my father didn't.

Love Sonnets: Taking the first two lines
of Zora Cross's 'Love Sonnets'

And, while I trembled by your side, one came
On wings of Wisdom, saying: 'I will show
You the place where the pink-and-greys nest,
Deep in a hollowed wandoo limb arched over
The Goldfields road; I will show you the place
Where the fox crosses that road to take new lambs,
Crossing back into the bush, weaving its way
Around 1080 baits dropped from the air,
Banned in America. The animal shaking violently,
Then dead. I will show you the quadruple flowering
Stems of the native grass trees along the fence-line
Just up from where the road dips towards the creek,
Their toothed strength a by-line for honey-eaters
And the comfort and blitheness of racist discourse.'

XXXI

We must look around upon our children dear,
Living through them, this present and that past;
And this is never more evident
Than when walking through old-growth forest;
The toddler ambling ecstatically the filtered light,
Rough-barked jarrah towering and closely packed,
Birds endemic to that place only
Darting around the undergrowth; his pleasure
Palpable, loggers nowhere nearby,
Though yellow markings on trunks,
Pink ribbon fluttering down the valley,
A 'grammar' of *his* children's barren landscape;
Denecourt's wild walks take us nowhere here,
A lust for aluminium undoing the propaganda.

XXXIV

O, could I count the stars that steer the night
Or chronicle the petals of all flowers,
I would divest myself of light
And live in your darkness: that car
Swinging out from behind the slow-moving
Truck, cutting into our path, the sharp
Whisper of its passing, exasperation
Whiplashing through bitumen . . . metal . . . resounding
Like the nightjar swooping between wandoos.
I thought: this, my last glimpse of all that matters,
Of all that's to come: not a word between us,
Lost to the corners of eyes: at such speed
The impact would leave all unsaid,
At home our children, wondering what'd happened.

LV

When by the borders of a crowded place,
I watch the breathing multitudes stream by,
And think of the *Seinfeld* episode
Where Jimmy says Jimmy does this
And Jimmy does that . . . the subject speaks
About itself in the third person, and among
The multitude — the subject — the speech
Of third persons lampoons the cross talk
And harmonic distortion, the futurist
Twirl of limbs in Central Station, the 'I would like . . .'
And 'you'll need' of ticket-sellers, the gratitude
A machine expresses over exact change. Jimmy
Likes New York — Jimmy's town — Jimmy
Leaves the station, walks the borders of shadow.

Novelty

Around the district occasional wedge-tailed eagles —
even, one afternoon, three, possibly four
on the sunset side of the mountain; yesterday
a first notarised — a massive wedge-tailed flying
from the mountain straight over the house, heading
south — the largest eagle I've seen, at least a ten-foot
wingspan, maybe fourteen, with a slow cruise
up the line of the gravel driveway, a rippling shadow
cast in multiple directions, as though the low winter sun
was just one of many hidden suns — it was, possibly,
a Roc — it scanned slowly from port to starboard,
surveying, though not predatorily. Its purpose
was not the assuaging of hunger, clearly.

Shortly before the appearance of the eagle,
walking the drive with my toddler Timothy,
we came across an owl pellet below the most distended
limb of a greyed dead York gum — the limb over the ochre
and stagnant waters of the driveway favoured by irrupting
birds — a perching place, a stopover between river and mountain:
black-shouldered kite, white-faced heron, egrets, cockatoos,
twenty-eights, magpies, crows — generally, larger birds.
At the exact point of passing over this event horizon
the eagle began its visual sweep, also, a Cessna was directly
above the eagle, though thousands of feet higher. It was
confluence and syzygy. The owl pellet on the ground below
suggests night birds perch in the dead tree branch also:

owls, tawny frogmouths, owlet nightjars. This was the pellet
of a large owl — a grey matting of skin and bone — a mouse —
and, strangely, a length of string wound like intestines
or an umbilical cord through the body waste. Ants were busy
divesting it. Ants have set up colonies at the drop zone.
It must be a semi-regular occurrence, one might hypothesise
from this. Timothy called the eagle a plane, and fixated
on the ants — slowing down with the encroachment of evening.

I am guessing it's a Boobook owl — I've often heard
the 'boo-book' anagrams at night, and have seen shapes flutter
heavily at dusk down near the shed. The Roc has left stories
and exclamatory prose — we are still talking about it — solidly — today.

Sympathy — Bogged

1. Front View

Heavy vehicle broad grin, tilted.
        Bogged — no traction.
Back wheels down to the axles.
        Bogged — no traction.
The artistry of submersion,
Barely detectable from front-
        On, dark clouds rolling overhead.
        Bogged — no traction.

2. Side View

Sympathise — he's down on his knees.
        Bogged — no traction.
Spirit level bubble ascends.
        Bogged — no traction.
Low-geared he tries to ease it out,
Semi-grip then centrifugal
        Rip, spinning wildly, flywheel blitz.
        Bogged — no traction.

3. Rear View

Deluge of Judgement — lateral.
            Bogged — no traction.
Incrementally dropping — cored.
            Bogged — no traction.
Illusion, merging verticals
And horizontals, tail-light sludge
        And embers — collapsed stars — buried.
            Bogged — no traction.

4. Bird's-Eye View: Coda

Black-shouldered kite hovers — faint light.
            Bogged — no traction.
Frayed tow-rope stretched between red cars.
            Bogged — no traction.
Ghost figures direct the action.
The triangle shifts, breaks angle.
        Old rope conducts — red on red, mud.
            Towed out — traction.

Wave Motion Light Fixed and Finished

Light carves a surface;
Light anneals fibres;
Light reflects and polishes;
Light collects in red gums;
Light infuses the river-mouth;
Light surfs rock and sand;
Light caught outside focuses in the studio;
Light's harmonics; Light's deletions;
Light's semi-tones of shadow;
silver parcels of sky-light; panels like prayer mats;
silver-leaf leaves flattened rolled out luminous ignition of solar
panels cloud formational reprise and a top-dressing finished glance;
ergo sum, ergo sunt, ergonomics of steel-pinned beauty,
Frida Kahlo strength, the saw bench, saw-light, wound
healing as wood planed to river loop and stretch, upwind downstream
filaments of trees reaching into salt-freshwater rendition, to walk
on black foil lift-off surface tension skip a beat
fish jump in largesse of cloud, tonnage of water vapour
as carved out old laws and coastal raiders
as fourteenths of a whole, holistically challenging to float above
a bed of wood, a bed of air, a bed of light, as solid as erosion from
southerlies cutting into hamlets and guilds,
a code, a tapping of branch on branch we might think
vaguely light Morse code this small part we can see at once
of any vision, any transmutation of heightened emotion, the variable
light of idea, sketch, rough, and finished product, artefact, item, example,
distillation . . . an economy of presence, an evidence of passing through the wa

of horizon, the highs and lows of occupation . . . silver nitrate tint, Polaroid
caught out before exposure, lightning-driven trees lit up like superstition, anatomy
interface grain reaching across planar quelling of spilt tea, spilt coffee,
blackbutt counteraction, storm-fallen revivification, as if each cell in its harmonic
is charging for renewal, the divan the ocean we slide into, nesting
chairs called back to the same spot to amplitude, sine wave
that lopes scansion bevelled edges tanged to ferrel and groove,
to sit and look out at imprints of rapture or haunting, luminous fire-wrought
hardened stock and buffer zone, delay contact consumed and melded
to carry out day-to-day activities, concentrate on one aspect of revelation,
a music emanates as light over ripples and echo-soundings
of wood density and rock density and water density and the sunset off-cuts
of light dampened, the temple stretched, this slow-time analysis of decompression,
emerging from within the element, the bends bring contract
and oxygen does something else, here the bends are absorbed, you flow
with them emergence, the night-eyes not seen as steel glints
a fine line, spirits of night falter on light borders withdrawing or creeping
into the vista, a front blown out, sleep bandwidth in the silent sound system,
the pin dropping so loud in distillation; pragmatically, light moves across the table,
pragmatically, light fills the wall behind the canvas, the floor and walls
light-heavy, light-drenched; changeable, flighty, instant, light thrills
the horizon, thrills the sharp lines
outside the halo, runs riot, and river flows on
and the furniture in the bedroom, living room, lounge room, dining room . . .
kettles; going out . . . work, a show, a walk . . . a sense of where things sit
stays with you, side-step, accommodate, meld . . . as seagull, osprey, sooty
oyster-catchers, criss-cross and throw up solar panels, throw up diffuse
maps of absolute light; in the land's curvature, the shark swims through
the territory of roo and wallaby, heavy-bodied cows light on their feet,
up to the river's edge, forests breathing moistly; the lamps shifts and haunted

trees emerge, or figures of the dispossessed — they can't be built out,
textured into the immensity of ocean and sky and headland,
low wattage of sunset driven up over rise, silhouette intensifying
where we walked, where all have walked out of memory,
taking sustenance out of the reconfigured picture,
having been there before and before; a line of herring
race the coastline, heavier fish sit close to the bottom, poised
on the edge of our seats, the table floats on silver air, the sky
made horizontal, the horizon a vertical line attaching
ceiling and floor — no vertigo comes with this, or searching out vertigo
it is a sonorous warmth of blended specificity: light peaking and dropping,
crests and troughs, concurrent and ecliptic,
the certainty of form when solar activity upsets the animals, confuses
bio-rhythms, the certainty of the shape waking to look out over the same space,
sunspots ripping through heath and forest, sizing canvas and coating
the hard dead growth, a form of rekindling
the ups and downs of days alone, days full of shadow, days burning with glare
and a brooding atmosphere, days becalmed, days where a memory
forced down below the surface, planes of light, bursts out
like caught sun, and then settles back into the dimensions
of the domestic, the pastoral: light transfigures, regenerates, blinds;
light is not to be taken for granted; light's properties grow
in the limestone caverns where we haven't seen, the sea connected
with where we stand, or sit, or spread ourselves out to float or hover
or petrify or sink down into surfaces below surfaces
and perspectives of light, thin membrane of land carved by seven waves
then seven waves and so on, on one side and lightly so on, on the other
more circumstantial though never casual the repetitions of wave motion,
river lappings carried against the banks against the skin-drum, against
Light's semi-tones of shadow;

Light's harmonics; Light's deletions;
Light caught outside focuses in the studio;
Light surfs rock and sand;
Light infuses the river-mouth;
Light collects in red gums;
Light reflects and polishes;
Light anneals fibres;
Light carves a surface . . .

Sounds of the Wheatbelt

The grasshopper roar is almost the locust roar
though not quite a swarming, just holding off
an issue of damp and dry, though intensity
of insect traffic as three-dimensionally tense
the eardrum of the paddock strains and a barking dog
is hoarse against the rustling electric scrum,
the whirr, the racket, the scratching and clicking,
attempt to flip upright, rotoring hover, Doppler
rush-by, hell-diver and sound-barrier imploder,
scissoring and slicing, smashing and crunching,
serrations pulling and parting, riffling carapaces
to expose the sound-makings, staccato
premonitions, signalling nightfall and drawn-to-lights,
heat seekers and seers of the heart's glowing beating outline,
unearthing and gnashing out to pincer
the bull by the horns, flutter as fine as the wings
that reflect the eye of the wagtail, sun's stimulation . . . wing-walking
along hotlines of nymphs and egg-layings,
feathers see-sawing down from cracked dead branches
where an arguing and jesting flock of galahs high-balls
into sunset, zips ripped down and jamming skin,
crows beak-twisting and drawing out the inevitable,
thick rustle of bobtail with just-enough acceleration
to get down below the flurry of wingsters,
incendiary consumers in a rush to get done,
such a short claim to our already accustomed ears . . .
threatening to conflagrate the crackling grasses.

Riding the Cobra at the York Show
(The Artificial Infinite)

Hoodwinked by the flat-lining, inside out
Silver lining of every absent cloud,
A clear day halo, a vulcanised rout
Of dust and eucalypt, diesels and loud
Stereos hyping up an eager crowd:
Addendum to truck and trailer, it rears
Up and contorts, hydraulically proud,
Eyes in the back of the head, cobra peers
Out into the hills and paddocks: it fears

Less with each scream. Down there — about to wake —
Snakes that wouldn't recognise it — dugites,
Gwarders, pythons, blind snakes . . . this clap-trap take-
All-before-it blow-in whiplash that skites
Loud enough to wake the dead, deny rites
Of belonging. Still, it rouses the prey
To come out into the open, reach heights
Once unimaginable; praise this lay
Society, almost too proud to pray.

Hooked elbow, steel lap-trap, drop-pod lock-down . . .
Centrifuge of senses and kinetics,
On the blow-out, rise up and twist, your frown
Looking down and out at the granite quirks
Of sunset ridges, peripatetics
Of ripening crops, glib orality

Of sideshow clowns, unravelling antics
Of object and shade . . . the finality
Of bent guns in shooting tents, reality

Sublimated and betrayed like roos caught
In a spotlight; centre of tension, soul
Lolling out of the mouth, memory fraught
With unresolved theologies, the roll
Of light and unction dipped in the blurred bowl
Of endolymph, the body osmotic;
This sharp arabesque as elemental
As Hyperion's car freaking parrots
And judges of the show's best: despotic!

So cedillas hanging heavy with bi-
Lateral agreement, torque and sentience
Weighed up in slowing, operator's wry
Perving as limbs unfold, his dependence
On post-rush joy hidden by a grimace:
Vertigo, obtuse valley-lift anchored
By hill's reprise . . . cobra lodged in conscience,
Iron-clad alibi, convalescing, coiled
Double helix, lime-lit, reloaded — bored.

Some: An Ode to the Partitive Article

Some burn-outs on asphalt stretch outside trig tables
Some galahs refuse to toe the line
Some solar cells gather waving lines of morphemes
Some striated pardalotes nidify just now, some shortly
Some spray booms disassociate, haze painted button quail
Some crop dusters plague the guy waving from his rooftop
Some bush bashers patiently tend some crops-in-the-bush you stay
        away from if you don't want to be shot
Some windmills shake down, rung on rung of saline accumulation
Some hubs on mallees mark driveways
Some samphire is salt bush in some necks of the clear-fell
Some wedgetail eagles harried by crows stay high above pasture
Some laterite conduits are County Peak
Some casuarinas are melaleucas are grevilleas are hakeas are acacias are
        eucalypts if you forget your guide book
Some poddy-dodgers are dodgers of law-makers and indulgers of flesh in-takers
Some sandhi are a(n) handy way of vowelling a wheat harvester
Some intermediaries focus specific causes for a decline
        in yellow skink numbers
Some wattles hold back flowering (sometimes)
Some farmers drive past three times in case they've missed catching you
Some lives are lost on crossroads
Some parishioners visit other people's churches, temples, mosques . . .
Some internees collect, collate and work the earth — friends
        turn enemies, encryption of fences . . .
        offspring on town council
Some new migrants settle on marginal land, push scrub

past breaking-point, fibro houses vacant now,
companies taking profits
Some fettlers save money and send it back home, some drink it in the town
saloon, rail now much diminished
Some kids at school say 'foreigners' will knife you in your sleep —
they marry the sisters of their enemies and have big families
Some kids sell tomatoes at roadside stalls, saying 'Buoni pomodori!'
Some prayers connect and others don't, all get played back,
are held to account
Some red-capped robins rip into our dark spots
and make light of them
Some polluted places are so beautiful
they make you weep buckets . . .

Wet Wood

Wet wood — I am trying to light a fire
        for warmth. In a few months
lighting a fire out here will be a crime —
        a serious crime.
                      Once,
when cooking on a Metters stove in summer,
        spark-arresters, long chimney,
and a certain amount of luck played out
        against total fire bans.

For cooking, you lit the fire before dawn,
        or after sunset . . . hot baths
maybe once a week — a copper
        heated on the stove top.
If a spark escaped and stayed illuminated
        in its chaotic arc down
to bone-dry stubble, it'd all go up,
        the house brought down
with paddocks, bush, roadside vegetation.
        The fire would roll over gravel
and singe words of damnation and exasperation
        spun out of neighbours' mouths.

So dry, there was no water to fight
        fires with anyway.
You could retreat into the muddy slurry
        of the house dam, and hope

you didn't succumb to smoke,
                scorched air.
                                        Later,
when the mains power came through,
                the risk of a spark
from the shed generator — 32 volts —
                was replaced by the risk
of powerlines whiplashing ignition
                in a high dry wind — 240 volts.

'We can't have war out here . . .'
                it was occasionally
argued . . . 'one explosion, one hot tracer,
                and we'd lose
everything . . .' So dry, it crackles
                with static, the blue flame
a 'living nightmare' . . .

                                        Wet wood —
I am trying to light a fire for warmth.
                In a few months
lighting a fire out here will be a crime —
                a serious crime.
While the wood is wet it's hard to spark
                a conflict. Though
we know how, how to burn
                the unburnable.

Forest Encomia of the South-West

1.

Head State Forester, my grandfather
surveyed jarrah and counted pines
tucked into the hardwood
as soft sell, short shrift,
quick-growing
turnarounds; watched fire
sweep across his fiefdom,
crosscut into ledgers,
health of that jarrah and marri,
blackbutt on the fringe,
named the fastidiousness
of his Sasanach wife
Anna Livia Plurabelle,
and made her Irish
where the convolution of sounds
was called 'the bush', and dances
at Jarrahdale were as far
away as the hospital.

Kinsella is a road and a forest.
Kinsella is an overlay.
Kinsella is a post-war boom-time
verging on the changing ways.
He died when I was a few years old.
He smoked heavily.

Was tall with a parched face.
My father took me to look at the absent signifier,
the hollow birth-right: the fire-tower,
the ever-ready batteries' cardboard cylinders
still below, the phone smashed by vandals.
Up the fire trail, on the granite summit,
hard-core partying place.
Arsonist incidentals' irony
too good to refuse as the lighter gloats
in high temperature and fuck, man, you've set it off,
can't stamp it out, let's get the fuck out of here.
They don't say a word, ever. But you've
met them in pubs. You've seen the spark
in their eyes, their hatred of forests.

The resinous hardwood I split with an axe
as if under the seared surface
it's seamed;
                    from a young age the off-cuts
of his bush upbringing — my father, *his* father —
a brother — an uncle — chopped another brother's
finger off — a dare on the chopping block —
and his father walloped the executioner.

Some family from County Wicklow,
foresters there,
foresters here,
a man's man . . .
and you're Claude's
grandson?
Surprising.

2.

Reportage? When
they came in at Ludlow
they cut the massive open-forest tuarts
and tried farming. That's the 1850s
and there's little talk
of Nyungar people in the forest,
though an artist tells me
there are Kinsellas who are blackfellas,
and I wonder why I've never met them,
heard of them. I want to find them,
for them to find me.

The sand-mining company
has the government in its pocket — this
is a barely renovated cliché —
and in the forest, police,
saying they'd be over the line
along with the dreadlocks and guitars
if the law told them to,
said all you can do
is watch the survey markers.
I ring lawyers. If they go outside
the allotted space . . . indigenous rights,
rare species, all are collated
in the effort to resist. Failure
allots expediency to the roadside camp
and issues of masculinity: locked on,
boys score points and tally arrests,

the forest goes under, girls
in dungarees call on the moon goddess,
and they move on.

3.

My father, long separated from the forests
of his birth, drives through the wooded country
just for the sake of driving. I like to go up
into the hills, he says. Just to drive.

4.

Surrounded by the paraphernalia of foresting
the cutting and tearing of bark is head over shoulder
in the pit, raining down flaky tears,
an electric rip — of the tongue,
taste not so unlike the taste we have of ourselves,
skin, flesh, chapels in a clearing,
wound sucked dry,
ice-skimmed water baptismally broken,
threads of mist as sunrises and sunsets
suffused are as much as we witness
on open plains, oceans;
never mind the pain
of working bullocks.

5.

Giving the finger to a logging truck
is giving the finger to small-town rage
against heritage imagined as consistency
and moral equilibrium, as connection,
as vacant spaces grind logic into woodchips
and the spout shoots out time sheets.

Giving the finger to a logging truck
is to make the barrelled weight of trunks shift
against the squared U-prongs of praise, offerings-up,
gimleted throats to chain and separate
from the better halves of self; in the blood,
the rush is a drink in a bar that trucks no ferals.

Giving the finger to a logging truck
is a shooting offence, and a get-busted-for-dope-
carrying offence, and a laying-open of the secret
places retribution comeback getting ahead
making a buck fuck the old-growth lock-up
pent-up release, the swerve of the big wheel

ratio to asphalt and hitch-hiker
stranger danger fallout.

6.

Mettle and impulse are group settlement
nano-probe Borg cube homesteads
rendering karri stands fused with paper

the good word is printed on,
anaphora in keeping accounts;
so lengthy the cordage,
building the State,
O liberty looked out upon
from the tall trees.

7.

Sustainable equals dispossession.
Sustainable equals clear-felling.
Sustainable equals selective picking out of infrastructure.
Sustainable equals dieback.
Sustainable equals balance of payments.
Sustainable equals nice floorboards in parliamentary metonymics.
    Go where you want with this.
Sustainable equals God at the top of the pyramid, logging companies the
    next rung down.
Sustainable equals the wood for the trees.
Sustainable equals the log in your eye, the splinter in your sister's.
Sustainable equals ochre rivers and a peeling-back of the layers
    of allegory — extended metaphors all the way to the sea.
Sustainable equals the widened highway and its support services' flow-on
    effect.
Sustainable equals the commiserating blocks on the forest's edge reaching
      into the forest bit by bit with the environmentally-minded
      eroding their privilege bit by bit.
Sustainable equals the forest-loving dope-grower who crushes the micro
    with every step,

as delicate and caring as they might be, introducing weeds as s/he
never would with prickly pear or rose, the rabbits loving
the tender shoots, O children of nature.
Sustainable equals dieback trod and trod through by effusing bushwalkers
infiltrated by bird calls — shocked into spirituality by the
weather calls of white-tailed black cockatoos.
Sustainable equals stars cut out around milling towns, forming the
southern cross
in nation-building recognition of later migrant influence.
Sustainable equals forest by any other name.
Sustainable equals election promises
come up trumps, couched in reassurances.

8.

It's so wet in there: wetter
than anywhere else. A deflected wet
that intensifies, gets under all cover.
In the ice cold you sweat,
and are we under the layers,
the canopy focusing
hard-hitting echoes
on every pore,
clasping undergrowth
too succulent, luring
you in where it's no drier.

9.

Extra-wide gravel roads
deep south so fire won't roll
as smoke so dense
you crawl
slower than through the worst fog
tightened windows preventing
not of the suffocating sting
you associate with those
you love most, love most
in the time left to you,
the pluming crown of flame
as much a vision
as you're going to get.

Leconte de Lisle's 'Le rêve du jaguar'
(The Jaguar's Dream)

Beneath dark mahogany trees, in the stagnant,
Humid air, saturated with flies, hang flowering
Lianas coiling up from vine stumps, lulling
The splendid and quarrelsome parrot,
The yellow-backed spider and wild monkeys.
Here is where the slayer of oxen and horses,
Sinister and weary, returns with measured
Steps along the mossy bark of old dead trunks.
On he goes, rubbing his muscular arched
Back, and, from the gaping jaw heavy
With thirst, a short, husky breath, a brusque
Twitch disturbs the great lizards, hot with midday
Fires, whose flight flashes across reddish grass.
In a hollow of the dark wood forbidden to the sun,
He sinks, stretched out on some flat rock;
With a large swipe of his tongue he shines his paws;
He blinks his eyes — sleep-dazed, golden;
And, in the illusion of his latent power,
Flicking his tail and with quivering flanks,
He dreams that in the middle of the green arbours,
With one leap, he sinks his liquid claws
Into the flesh of startled and bellowing bulls.

Arthur Rimbaud's 'Le bateau ivre'

As I was drifting down impassive Rivers,
I no longer felt guided by the haulers:
The yowling Redskins had taken them as targets,
Having nailed them naked to painted stakes.

I didn't give a damn for any of the crews,
Carrying Flemish wheat or English cottons.
When, along with my haulers, these quarrels were done with,
The Rivers let me float downstream as I wished.

Last winter, in the furious lapping of tides,
Deafer than the minds of children,
I ran! And the unmoored Peninsulas
Never experienced more triumphant turmoil.

The storm blessed my nautical stirrings.
Lighter than a cork I danced on waves
They call eternal breakers of victims,
Ten nights, without missing the shore-lights' ludicrous eyes!

Sweeter than flesh of sour apples to children,
The green water spilled into my pinewood hull,
And cleansed me of vomit and blue wine stains,
Tossing aside rudder and anchor.

And from that moment, I bathed in the Poem
Of the Sea, a milky infusion of stars devouring
Green azures; where — flotsam enraptured and sallow —
A pensive drowned man sometimes goes down;

Where, suddenly dyeing the blueness, deliriums
And slow rhythms beneath the gleamings of day,
Stronger than alcohol, greater than our lyres,
The bitter russets of passion ferment!

I know skies cracking open with lightning, waterspouts,
Undertows and currents: I know evening,
Dawn ecstatic as a flock of doves,
And I have sometimes seen what man has believed he saw!

I have seen the sun low, tainted with mystical horrors,
Illuminating distended purple coagulations,
Just like actors in ancient dramas
Waves rolling into distance the frisson of shutters.

I have dreamt the green night with dazzled snows,
Kiss rising slowly to the gaze of seas,
The circulation of extraordinary saps,
And the yellow-blue stirring of singing phosphorus!

I have followed, for entire months, the swell
Attacking the reefs with its hysterical bitching,
Without dreaming that the luminous feet of Marys
Might force shut the jaws of gasping Oceans!

I have, you know, struck astounding Floridas
That blend with flowers the eyes of panthers
In human skin! Rainbows stretched like bridles
On murky green herds, beneath the seas' horizon.

I have seen huge marshes fermenting, traps
Where a whole Leviathan rotted in the bulrushes!
Downfalls of water in the midst of a becalmed sea,
And the horizons collapsing into abysses!

Glaciers, silver suns, pearly waves, embered skies!
Hideous strandings in the depths of muddy gulfs
Where massive serpents devoured by crawlers
Spill with a black stench from twisted trees.

I would have liked to show children those gilthead bream
Of the blue wave, those golden fish, those singing fish.
Foaming flowers rocked my wanderings
And ineffable winds at moments lent me wings.

Sometimes, a martyr weary of poles and zones,
The sea whose sobs lulled my rolling,
Lifted shadowy flowers with yellow suckers
Toward me, and I stayed there, like a woman kneeling . . .

Almost an island, hurling up on my shores
The squabbles and crappings of screeching blank-eyed birds.
And I sailed, until, across my frail ropes,
Drowned men retreated downwards into sleep!

But now I, boat entangled in cove-hair,
Pitched by the hurricane into the birdless ether,
Whose water-drunk carcass the Monitors and Hanse yachts
Would not have fished up again;

Free, smoking, risen from purple mists,
I who pierced the sky's reddening wall
Which bears, exquisite jam to superior poets,
Lichens of sunshine and azure snot,

Who would escape, stained with electric demi-moons,
A crazy plank escorted by black seahorses
When Julys, with hammer blows, collapsed
Ultramarine skies into burning funnels.

I who trembled at groans travelling fifty leagues:
The rutting ardour of Behemoths and turgid Maelstroms,
Perpetual spinner of blue stillnesses,
I pine for Europe with its ancient parapets!

I have seen archipelagos of stars! and islands
Whose delirious skies are unlocked to the sailor:
Do you sleep and exile yourself in these fathomless nights,
Million golden birds, O Strength of the future?

But, truly, I've wept too much! Dawns are devastating.
Every moon is appalling and every sun bitter:
Acrid love has engorged me with intoxicating torpors.
O let my keel rupture! O let me sink into the sea!

If I long for any water in Europe, it's the black
Cold pool where toward fragrant twilight
A child crouching full of melancholy,
Releases a boat frail as a May butterfly.

I can no longer, bathed in your languors, O waves,
Sail in the wake of the cotton-bearers,
Nor sweep through the pride of flags and pennants,
Nor swim beneath the hideous eyes of hulks.

The Sands of Djarlgarro Beelier

for Trevor Jamieson and Noel Nannup

1. CONCEPTION

We don't like to ask, but I'd guess it was
in the house bought for the purpose. Bateman
Road, just up from Bateman's Farm — a colonising
space. A bike-ride from the paperbarks, the thin white
riverbeach, the grey jetties, seagulls cormorants pelicans.
Sharks were seen that far up. Sharks in the *Canning*,
as I first heard it named — in the womb, listening.
Speedboats would come and introduce me to irony,
the violence of the outdoors, waves wearing
away at the river's walls. The city starting
to close in around, the plentiful made sparse —
river prawns netted at night, lights singeing
tanned waters, then gone. There were masses
of blue manna crabs and mulloway and the river
thronged with fertility. I was conceived
with limestone foundations between flesh
and black sand. Edging to grey, white
by the river's edge lit up by the close moon.
When the seed bit the egg and I cried out.
The river's business. It's the river we ask.

2. Birth

I was born in the South Perth Hospital
not far from where Djarlgarro Beelier and Derbarl Yerrigan
diverge. I became where the rivers branch.
I was taken home to the banks of the 'tributary'.
The water flowed down from the hills, down from forests
and farmlands. I was taken up to the watershed
before I could talk or walk — early, it was my in-between
place. As soon as I was old enough, I was carried
up to the wheat. Up through jarrah into wandoo.
I went up from water and sand to stone and clay,
up from pelicans and bream to parrots and echidnas.
But I was born near the fork of those rivers, where black sand
meets white sand, where blind snakes and sandgropers
burrow their way and water rats range across meeting-places
and bloodworms work the mud, the summer sun glinting.

3. Umbilical Cord

I imagine my cord was stolen not far
from where the 'Canning' and 'Swan' rivers diverge, branch.
Taken to the incinerator. My first cremation, my ash,
my mother's ash, floating high into the atmosphere
then drifting down on riverfoam, on lawns
of half-dead buffalo grass, on Bristile clay roofing tiles,
on black sand, on yellow sand, on the white sand
of riverbeaches edged by paperbarks with blisters
ready to burst with watery sap, with goodness.

4. First Steps

I lifted and stepped quickly before falling
a few blocks from Djarlgarro, a measure of houses
where tracks had waved through banksias and marris,
a short walk from where the river bends to continue up to the hills,
a moment from where a spur leads off to a cul-de-sac,
a semi-dead-end, where a creek feeds Djarlgarro through reeds.
The snakes were there. That's where they moor boats
away from the weather and build houses to the water.
Bamboo. Bateman's Farm. The history it enforces.
Up on my feet, I walked the Axminster carpet,
then out onto lawn, then into the black sand
which covered my steps. I observed
the ant lion, and later the lacewing,
plentiful about the river — down through banksias,
marris, onto the white sand, into the salty water,
onto the mud flats, the fresh creek water running over,
mingling, diluting. The reeds hid clutches of duck eggs.
The sand hid me. I planned where I'd go. Where
the sea water joined the hill's water, the creek water.
Where salt and fresh waters meet. Where salt water
would meet salt water when I was older.
And I was sad for all that my birthing hid.

Bushfire Sun

Howard Taylor

Smoke clouds thickens diffuses palls chokes spreads plumes swarms smothers
Smothers swarms plumes spreads chokes palls diffuses thickens clouds smoke
Smoke clouds thickens diffuses palls chokes spreads plumes swarms smothers
Smothers swarms plumes spreads chokes palls diffuses thickens clouds smoke
Smoke clouds thickens diffuses palls chokes spreads plumes swarms smothers
Smothers swarms plumes spreads chokes palls diffuses thickens clouds smoke
Smoke corona radiance halo haze   haze halo radiance corona smoke
Smoke corona radiance halo   halo radiance corona smoke
Smoke corona radiance   radiance corona smoke
Smoke corona   Orange   corona smoke
Smoke   hue of the Planckian locus   smoke
Smoke corona   Orange   corona smoke
Smoke corona radiance   radiance corona smoke
Smoke corona radiance halo   halo radiance corona smoke
Smoke corona radiance halo haze   haze halo radiance corona smoke
Smothers swarms plumes spreads chokes palls diffuses thickens clouds smoke
Smoke clouds thickens diffuses palls chokes spreads plumes swarms smothers
Smothers swarms plumes spreads chokes palls diffuses thickens clouds smoke
Smoke clouds thickens diffuses palls chokes spreads plumes swarms smothers
Smothers swarms plumes spreads chokes palls diffuses thickens clouds smoke
Smoke clouds thickens diffuses palls chokes spreads plumes swarms smothers

Lexical Spectrum 1

Sine Macpherson

I'm as specific as you.
Fifth band down, right edge:
six bars of colour. I won't name
the colours, you can. I count
the apertures of King's College Chapel,
the number of bricks in walls
while waiting at the doctor's.
As a child I collected nouns.
This spectrum disorder
is as precise as misunderstanding.
Without the right reader
it can't be scanned as some
might intend: but the gaps
between colours I read
as the field I have walked across,
the mountain I will climb, the dragon-
fly that isn't a mayfly,
are recorded as 'aims' in my
journal (and/or diary).
Where I have been is forgotten
as I don't record that. Not
in the same way. But the weight
of my steps leaves a mark,
and the lexical takes stock.

White Painting

Nyapanyapa Yunupingu

All I have is respect
and curiosity
and gratitude
that whiteness
is being returned
to intactness
as sewn and webbed
into glare   reflection
refraction   collector

of ancestors I might
hear if invited
to hear stretching
back into our Oneness
our mutual belonging
or choices of bridges
taken or turned
away from   listening
listening

celestial as translation's
stretch across radiance
and what takes us
inside out across
another's span
of making of surface

like the fourth person
an extra tense
or my trying to make
speech without articles
but rich in names

rich in names and actions
brighter even
than treeskins
bearing white
casting white shadows
where white is quiet,
a totality, a tessellation.

Ganyu — the universe

Gulumbu Yunupingu

This is the universe.

I can translate. In this, I surprise myself.

But a quota of wonder is something.

Knowledge, which I don't have, is another.

> But formation and dark matter
> and light we might even think
> of as conventional transpire to
> make it easy. *Wherever* we come
> from. Which is of importance
> because the universe mapped
> from country will know special
> and unique aspects of itself.
> Formations and endings. The
> *between* formulation. Where we
> go before birth and after death.
> Where *we* fit into *us*, and where
> rock and air and all days and
> nights meet. And are made.
> Unmade. Remade. I know this.

I can translate. In this I surprise myself.

This is the universe.

Untitled J04

Karl Wiebke

So let me tell you how it is from the zone.
I have spent much time in the zone.
I have written reports and sent them out
to Karl but haven't heard back. I think
he thinks I'm too weird when I am in the zone
he has laid out offered prompted drawn up
from the surface, making light of terrain

that in truth runs yellow rivers, off-fire
just below, small greenish patches
that never make fields but promise
so much — I linger too long in such places,
hope for a revelation of tranquillity,
but it never comes, or danger is so close
that I don't take the chance and move on.

In the zone all ridges are encounters
with conscience. Are encounters with prospects
of silence and noise, of calm and restive
echoes. The bell ring solidified. It is a terrifying
if pleasurable prospect. I sense you all
looking down on me as I make the journey
overland. I live off its land. Travel light.

Through the centre from north to south,
then east to west, or zigzagging. I am often
lost. Being lost brings loss but makes
for new awareness. I find metaphors.
I do not understand language that's not
figurative. I find Biblical punctuation
but no God. But there might be many gods

between ridges, always escaping as I scale
another challenge, come to grips with profile.
I pass colours through the spectrograph.
The flame lights up with mineral deposits.
Beneath crests of the waves pigment
consolidates. Layers accrete on something solid,
though I have sand feet when I scale the largest

ridges. The lulls are calm and melodious,
but I favour the high places where winds
riff off edges. Up there, it's all feedback.
But it's the sum of its parts, the zone,
and it's up to you to step in and risk
all: discovery is work, Overlanders:
make each step add up to more and more.

The Travelling Eye — a piece of 'op. cit.'

on Bridget Riley's 'Nineteen Greys'

'The eye can travel over the surface in a way parallel to the way it moves over nature. It should feel caressed and soothed, experience frictions and ruptures, glide and drift. One moment, there will be nothing to look at and the next second the canvas seems to refill, to be crowded with visual events.'

— Bridget Riley

```
grey   grey   grey   grey   grey   grey   grey   grey   grey   grey   grey   grey
grey   grey   grey   grey   grey   grey   grey   grey   grey   grey   grey   grey
grey   grey   grey   grey   grey   grey   grey   grey   grey   grey   grey   grey
grey   grey   grey   grey   grey   grey   grey   **grey** grey   grey   grey   grey
grey   grey   grey   grey   **grey** grey   **grey** grey   grey   grey   grey   grey
grey   grey   grey   grey   **grey** **grey** **grey** grey   grey   grey   grey   grey
grey   grey   grey   grey   Print moves not eye.          grey   grey   grey   grey
grey   grey   grey   grey   Print elides nature.          grey   grey   grey   grey
grey   grey   grey   grey   Print warps green ovals       grey   grey   grey   grey
grey   grey   grey   grey   **grey**  and multiplies,     grey   grey   grey   grey
grey   grey   grey   grey   **grey**  drained to grey.    grey   grey   grey   grey
grey   grey   grey   grey   grey   **grey** grey   **grey** grey   grey   grey   grey
grey   grey   grey   **grey** grey   **grey** **grey** grey   grey   grey   grey   grey
grey   grey   grey   grey   **grey** **grey** grey   grey   grey   grey   grey   grey
grey   grey   grey   grey   **grey**  Bend and twist      grey   grey   grey   grey
grey   grey   grey   grey   **grey**  far to faint edges, grey   grey   grey   grey
grey   grey   grey   **grey** Eye stuck to surface.        grey   grey   grey   grey
grey   grey   grey   grey   Eye drained and satiate.      grey   grey   grey   grey
grey   grey   grey   grey   Eye crowds mad to centre.     grey   grey   grey   grey
grey   grey   grey   grey   grey   grey   **grey** grey   grey   grey   grey   grey
grey   grey   grey   grey   grey   grey   grey   grey   grey   grey   grey   grey
grey   grey   grey   grey   grey   grey   grey   grey   grey   grey   grey   grey
grey   grey   grey   grey   grey   grey   grey   grey   grey   grey   grey   grey
grey   grey   grey   grey   grey   grey   grey   grey   grey   grey   grey   grey
```

To Boullée (1993) by Michael Dan Archer

When severe weather hit and there was an instant need for shelter we didn't hesitate to stand in the lee of *To Boullée*. Its granite was of the hills we had left behind, and its architecture fitted our needs perfectly. We inhabited it as the idea of Newton inhabits the unbuilt *Cénotaphe à Newton*. We made a mythology of its lines and grain and returned to our roots. We marvelled at the functional nature of the cross cut into its flesh, the anchor and hull of the rock-bed. Firm in the face of the storm, it nonetheless floated as if there wasn't a worry in the world. But when the storm had passed and we stepped out from its influence, we feared we'd been possessed by the monumental, the fast slow passing of time.

The Many Moods of Marilyn,
à la Andy Warhol

1.

Solemn as stony
enclaves closed with evening;
late light lingering.

2.

Your eyes adjusting
to her eyes so accustomed
to ideas of night.

3.

So! Razzle-dazzle
spotlight enfilade colour
splash in the tabloids.

4.

The sickness is more
than her publicist lets on;
she eats oranges.

5.

That guy has brought out
the devil in her — who would
have thought — that nice girl!

6.

Would Griffiths have cast
her as *black* or *white* given
a rebirthed nation?

7.

Sing Happy Birthday
Mr President and you'll
embarrass myself?

8.

I love this goddess —
I have seen her in the fields
the wide world over.

9.

We all have off-days
when a kiss lingers longer
than a bold kisser.

10.

'Cool' requires this.
You've got to have starting points.
Diverse fetishes.

Burning Eyes

Burning eyes that peer out of a dry crop at night,
shape the seasons and our response —
twin sparks that light the driest stalks
fail to flame, won't combust where you pass.

I see them each night driving home, lit up
by headlights — fox, cat, a rare marsupial
frozen between rows, magnetised by the car's approach.
So frequent over the last fortnight that a pall

of doubt has gripped me: an afterimage I carry
from that first encounter, reigniting in time,
same point every night. I can't bring myself to vary
the plan, to alter the variables; the scheme

of sight, of shine and glint, has trapped
us both. The dry is drying out towards harvest.
Not a vestige of moisture in the stalks — either way,
burning eyes will pass out, lack fuel to conflagrate.

Something must break. I will go away before night
comes to pass as day, or day eats far into night
with burning eyes that peer out of a dry crop.
It's the eclipse of content where compulsion stops.

Write-off

Night drives home are always fraught
and an eye has to be kept out for kangaroos
and even emus, sometimes foxes and often rabbits
plus owls and tawny frogmouths that swoop
across the parabola of headlights. For a lifetime
I've avoided striking anything large on this road,
though the car grille has choked on insects, has glutted
with plague-season locusts. Picking wrecked bodies
from filaments of radiator, even mangled into one body
with many more legs than genetically encoded, you realise
how large each death will always be. But it seems easier
to forget about than a medium-sized death when windscreen
catches tawny frogmouth and deflects into pitch-black sheets
hung between trees that bleed a phosphorescent orange,
mimesis of the car's disturbing aura, sentinels to body-
counts not added up when cars pass in morning light,
maybe night's carcasses already lifted by foxes
and carted off to veiled dens. This calibrating
of death obsesses me driving home late, keeping
owl-eyes sharp; is shattered when a grey kangaroo
bounds straight out at high speed from the forest;
I swerve to put the balance right and it's there again,
in front of me, a temporal anomaly that slows
world down to words — 'Brace! We're going to hit!' —
followed by impact, radiator meeting fan, fragmenting
into manifold and grinding out valves, cylinders —
flip of carcass past windscreen, over curve of roof,

into the aftermath of passing, wake of darkness, a sickly
tail-lit epilogue of care and obsession. What *are* prayers
really worth to the damaged, to the dead? Prayer is only
about the living, out there, out here, where death is the *only*
conversation. And to glide, brakeless, steering gone,
into an amorphous aloneness, an accident that could go
from bad to worse. To halt without order, without hope,
the car a write-off for what it's worth. And then out
of silence, shots fired in the forest, roos driven out
to escape hunters. Spotlights and dogs that chase
glimmers of eye-light in darkest dark. I know *that* dark —
it's *different*, and fear gives it no special name. I ask
my daughter to lie low in the back of the wreck —
young women can't be seen where there's no escape —
and I try to flag down a passing car. None stops,
intermittent as they are, but I am grateful the hunters
haven't emerged from the forest to check things out. A guy
with dreadlocks pulls up in a truck and relays a message
for help. In dark silence I wait with my daughter — we wait
and listen for roos' heartbeats, for the echo of the dead roo's
heart against shots fired in the dark. I tell her that my childhood
was loud with the pounding of roo hearts, that harm
doesn't mean harm will follow, and that belief works
faster than prayer. Help arrives. We push the wreck
off into a ditch as hunters emerge alert to a frisson
of life in death, mingling of metal and flesh. Spotlights
shine down on the wreck, on rescuers, on us. They rev engines
in triumph, ignoring roo hearts — small, medium-
sized, and large — beating rapidly about us, about them;
louder and brighter than engines, than spotlights.

Yellow

Tim has been filed
in Yellow Faction
at school. He is frustrated
and angry: he wants to be in
Red Faction, especially for the Cross Country,
which even five year olds train for in the Bush.
Character building. Robust. Preparatory.
I take him out to the garden
where I have piled the spent broad-bean stalks,
grey ropes of pea vines,
dead clumps of wild oats,
for a quick burning-off. We are
making ash for the next generation,
I tell him. The fire whips about in the cold
late autumn easterly. It should cut apart
the flames but incites them. Tim,
analytical as always, notes the colour of flame
and distance of colour from the fuel. The orange
and yellow flames furthest away, linger longer,
waver. I say: see, yellow is fast,
and yellow is the colour of the sun,
it is the body of the flames, orange
is the colour of the sun, it is the body
of flames. But Tim is also suspicious
of orange. When he hears a slow ballad
sung in French by, say, Piaf, he says: I don't
like it, it makes me see orange in my head.

He and I, from a distance, consider
the waverings of orange and yellow. He
interrupts the burn-down — smoke making day
night, and wisps of ash fluttering about
like something good — and says: fire
is red too and red is a great colour,
and the flames closer to what's burning
are almost blue. Blue is the fastest colour.
Inside the sun is the blue of our souls.
All other colours are fed by blue
and it makes us fast.
                              A few days ago,
during a sun shower, Tim said that raindrops
don't let some colours of the spectrum
through. Or even let them exist, like indigo,
which *must* be in the fire too.

Reverse Anthropomorphism

These birds — western flyeaters — are sizing
me up, making me within their own image,
moi-même, at least for the purpose of hunting.
Through glass, I watch them target their prey,
insects in the temporal zone of the verandah:

one flyeater darts out to seize an insect flyer,
then returns to watch his companion do the same.
The whole time they both keep an eye on me. *Moi-même*.
I connect with them in no way. No displacement
to fill the page: no female pushing a pram

full of letters, 'protecting the male'. Empirically,
they are male *and* female. It seems they perform
the *same* tactics, the same roles when hunting. Role-play?
Who am I to say? Some *would* say it's a matter
of knowing what to look for. *Moi-même*.

This is not a rare experience, it happens most days.
We have grown familiar. Don't mistake my indifference
for their indifference, or their relaxation
for a reflection of mine. We do not share.
Though I am touched that they are near.

And they manage to get done what they
need to get done. It's rich pickings
near where I sit, separated by the glass window,
insects making their own conversations,
losing lives. *Moi-même*. Role-play.

Hyperbole

Patois of the shredder,
shoddy skinner, demi-
pruner of roadside vegetation.
Poète engagé, ha! I pursue data,
inform my protest,
wrest lyrics from the brutal,
but the name of this rotator,
psychopathic cutter,
is hidden, encoded.

Travelling, I have caught
its progress, high-pitched
whirring, nerve destroyer,
too often — a seasonal
assignation, slasher
moment from which
the ghost-self emerges
tattered as living
and dead flesh mixed.

Truth is, I know
the operators, know
the work they crave: a call,
a few hours, a shire
pay-cheque. Just enough.
Today we flayed the garden.
At smoko we ribbed and jibed,

exaggerated the assets
of celebrities.

Mostly, that cutting whirr.
Mostly, the screeching banshee.
Mostly, the screaming ab-dabs
this machine induces.
Short-tempered
with the kids. I hear
this — it is said among friends.
For their sakes, also,
I protest, *poète engagé*, ha!

Resurrection Plants at Nookaminnie Rock

They're full-blown in their early spring
rush — pincushions a fakir's bed of nails
so soft to tread on, so easy to make false
comparisons by, and all the baggage *that* carries —
rest-break on a granite slab looking out over
the island sea of scrub shaded with formations
beneath a green lagoon's surface. It's what we
bring to the apogee before the drying-off,
dead crunch beneath our feet as rock-
dragons wake to the heat, and emphatic
belief that the dead will stay dead
and there will be no lift, no rebirth,
wherever you come from, whatever
you believe. Step carefully around these
wreaths hooked into granite sheen, holdalls
for a soil-less ecology, a carpet you know
would say so much more if your boots
were off and skin touched life brought
back, restored, gifted, bristling with death
because death is the most alive district
to inhabit. We could say so much more
                if only we had the time

Zoo Visits

He polished his car to a shine, he kept
a 'clean machine' inside and out, but down
from 'up north', the red dirt would stay
in the seams of doors, around the fittings.
A detailing of distance. A truth unto itself.

What to do with us, having travelled
so far — the access-visit conundrum, divorced
bloke's existential crisis. Kids aren't going
to live on feelings alone for an afternoon,
they want entertainment. Time is action.

The zoo excursion undoes its own irony —
the cages more than conceits, more than
allegories of maintenance and child support.
The babies of most species cling to their
mothers, and that's got to hurt. The smell

is so prevalent — we called it 'a stink',
the kind we gave off when badly behaved
and told off: a fear reaction. We were brave
leaning in through iron bars thick as Dad's arms,
knocking at the armour of the rhinoceros,

as wagtails picked insects off. Could it feel
their delicate feet? Its horn, worn down
to a stump, looked anything but mythical.

Rough skin fascinated us — the elephant's,
the hippopotamus rolling in its baby bath.

The fairy penguins launched from their castle
into a moat of fast food, and that was a talking
point. Penguins and Coke cans. Magical. Like
pythons in glass boxes or the smoking gorilla.
Time is action. And our dad glanced at his

watch out of anticipation. We didn't get that.
We were too busy making metaphors. The mini
railway wound its way around the heartlands.
Safari. The sound of species lost since then.
Zoological gardens. Family crisis centre.

The polar bear mauled someone who jumped
into its green waters. It leapt off its white ledges
bothered by no melt, ate, and covered its bloody
black nose. It happened before and after Dad
talked of its power. He liked the bears. And the cats.

He wanted us to like them. The big animals.
The big dads. Keep away from the edge,
he said in a way that meant more to us than
an excursion; than entertainment; than time.
Than the car he polished to a red dirt shine.

from Sea Shanties

WRECK AT COOGEE BEACH (1905–)

When Mum swam
the belly of the wreck
keelhauled over periwinkles
sand glowed where abattoir blood ran,
secrets of electricity spilled — power plant
perched on rocks overhead.
The deck closer to the sand,
        closer to the sand.
Gulls thick about the bowsprit.

Clinker hull, jackass barque,
carried cables for the overland telegraph;
made us who we are, in part — brothers
of the sand; rush to discover
where waves lap and storms
lash embryos of flotsam — whiting
and garfish at the deeper end,
octopuses gripping a broken stern.
The deck closer to the sand
        closer to the sand.
Gulls thick about the bowsprit.

When the *Omeo* broke its moorings
within the Sound, gale lashed
its aged body — that Mum might swim
her childhood again, write
the wreck as folklore; and we might
swim away or play the sand or lose
all thoughts of inland.
The deck closer to the sand
        closer to the sand.
Gulls thick about the bowsprit.

With all these tricks: *watch me! watch me!*
dive into sheltered waters, dive
where sea filled with effluent,
where sharks dizzied in bloody fluid;
let backwashed footprints
push up to reset perfect
sandy pictures, lit by kelp.
The deck closer to the sand
        closer to the sand.
Gulls thick about the bowsprit.

What I saw off Cheynes Beach

Seeing the black eyes of white pointers
some people want to poke them, to take these sea-
giants out with one small finger, 'defensive'
mastery greater than dragging

sperm whales in from the continental
shelf, those old Norwegian chasers
cutting through a whale slipstream,
the passages they know. So, at five
years old I stand on the warped

white sands of the beach, holidaying,
looking out into the bay at the flagged
carcasses of whales, mountains in the blue-black
ocean, disturbed like a split lip spitting
froth and fear, bobbing though so lifeless

I wonder what living is, sand too cold
beneath your feet, too cold in my long pants
and windcheater, the stench of flensing
and boiling down, teeth piled high,
seawater and blood and spermaceti

of the whaling station — reason for the town —
reason for posturing against the French,
an American connection from the beginning
they wished to make, filling the oil-lamps
of readers in cities around the globe.

Seeing the black eyes of white pointers
I wonder if they are one-eyed, orbicular
to the one side, to keep an eye out,
thrusting up on to the dead whales, side-
swiping jaws ripping skin and blubber

and I know then blood comes out of the dead
though it flows differently — I've already
cut myself severely — and the dark ocean
makes a different viscosity, an attracting
and diluting flow that is scent for sharks

to follow in, to rasp atmosphere over great gills
as they emerge like dolphins, but ample and rough
and with a new take on grace: who is to say,
this beautiful flesh-death, death in death,
so energised as they bite the air, our seeing.

All of me, all of Mum, and all of Dad
would fit into one of those white pointers,
giant finned barrels propelling teeth,
but I don't think that at the time,
on the shore, looking out at the blue-black-red

collars of blood, the growing number
of sharks, the glut and the feast and the strange
angles of biting and tearing and looking at me
not so far away but far away from shark mind
so single-mindedly completing its plan,

its awareness, its line of thought: the news
I will tell the following year when I start school,
my grandfather in the spotter plane, the thrill,
the chase, the history of harpoons and the anger
it will make in me and the blood it will fill

me with that's not red but froths with history
and witness and a dull science that quells fear
and vengeance even though my brother
will surf where surfers are taken, are snatched,
all of them saying, 'leave them be,

these great creatures', the driven and logical
giants who know their own company
and the cartilaginous nature of ocean
so solid and flexible and churned up
with all that we call matter, all

that post-Enlightenment posturing
we laugh at and over in our secular
worship, those large blips on the sonar,
those seeing black eyes of white pointers.

MEGAMOUTH SHARK

'About the Shark, phlegmatical one'
— Herman Melville

Should we be grateful they're not claiming
it as art, but as science? Or are they smugly
doubling up — the art of preservation the boon
of research? Megamouth, so rare it wasn't recorded
as science until 1976, day-time deep dweller
off the continental shelf to rise at night to a lesser
depth, to graze screeds of plankton we barely
register? So much for autonomy and agency
in the great body of water. Megamouth, 'rescued'
from death in shallows to depthless formalin, embalmed
within stainless-steel tank-of-the-dead, necropolis
aquarium so shiny and technical, with portholes
for us to peer through, its saucer eyes staring out
with a vision we can't configure, though the designer
can. The electric pump to keep preservative circulating
is eternal as power and its grid, as the toxic ocean
pulsing in the harbour. New centrepiece of the maritime
museum, its sails parsing the stiff sea breeze. Comparisons
are fuel for the patronising, and I can't help but think
this tank and its inhabitant are prescient fulfilment
of *Dune*, a pox on emperor houses of curators
and scientists, this Guild Navigator the benign

encapsulation of Edric shrouded in orange gas,
so distorted to outside eyes, plotting the courses of ships
through space without collision, devastation like anchor
lines and fishing nets, incidentals that make evidence
for our bemusement that such a beast could go unnoticed.
It offends us. There's agony in its scanning eye, its tiny
filtering teeth set in that gaping mouth, caught perversely
wide, a universal fellatio, opened to make it look more
than shark enough; and even science will realise
that it's undead, its 'ka' and 'ba' fixed and lost
in equal measure, the flow of fluid not even providing
an optical illusion, no 'weighing of the heart' beyond
the heartlessness of curiosity,
eschatology of display.

BLUE-RINGED OCTOPI

To hunt shores at night evokes a word we lack:
as *greater* frustrates the *lesser*, both having deadly
bacterial bites: the painless nip that makes paralysis
look inward though wide awake, watching your
tranquillity of demise. This isn't purely fact
collated from texts, but first-hand news: hand
touching the hand that touches the skin and agitates
a calm rockpool near mangroves to rings of bright
blue that mesmerise: liquid eyes of peacock tails.
Dying mixes metaphors, lays you out flat on the sand.
Welded mouth-to-mouth. Twenty-four hours,
a single breath. Not a breath to be had outside
the host's, breathless you give nothing back.
A marriage against convention and Nature.
That's your brother at twelve saying, 'Watch it move!',
flattened swirls across needles and jags of rock,
eight small legs that collect a space to hold
the pulsing head. Inkless inscription warning
small boys it will strike fingers through water
bending with the sun. Blue wedding rings.
And waiting for an electric shock that never
manifests, to pass through body unto body,
my pulling him away to break the shock.
You rarely feel the bite. And too late
if you do, as there's no cure but breath.

And repeated in cold southern waters, where
the *lesser* lurks in bottles and shells, neat beak
that rips a tiny crab apart, vacuuming flesh. The swell
incites rockpools, and tides bring on the scuttle.
To treasure such poisons — tetrodotoxin, maculotoxin —
the child who picks over innocence, loves risk,
loves fear, half-lulled by the ravaging of that great
amnion, the ocean. Or surrounded by mangroves
up north where it's hot and putrid and salty, where
infection sets into the smallest cut — mangroves'
false sense of security, mudflats stretching out as far
as tides can ever go — blue-ringed octopi lying low
in brine tepid with waiting. Hungry but shy.

THE MERRY-GO-ROUND BY THE SEA
(GERALDTON, WESTERN AUSTRALIA)

in memoriam Randolph Stow

It's beneath the ficus tree, umbrella
against the breadth of the sea,
but the harbour hedges bets anyway,
and foreshore build-up is profligacy.

Facsimile to start with, fixed
paradox to hear closer the rush
of westerlies, the curl of breakers
around the point. Hustle of town.

It varied for each of us — centrifugal
or centripetal certainty, according
to our different natures. And the giddy
fascination with where explorers

go to be lost to others, overwhelmed
by bones and light and themselves.
And light through branches, glimmering
of the changeable surface is all here.

It's the technology of wrecks: the metal
of cannons, astrolabes, and coins of realms.
An antenna charged by the young, like
a raw colonial future. Blind sunset.

Stopped mid-spin, can it hold its charge,
anchored by a plaque? Son of the town
writes centres, pole we spin around.
His story is our story retold?

Some decline the offer. Some
skip stones out over the water,
a murky leaden colour. Others listen
hard to shells that stay silent,

if they've ever spoken. We've never
felt more alone than swinging on the merry-
go-round with strangers to balance
the compass, making the rules.

I saw an osprey on the foreshore
not far away: its standing shape
not glamorous as in flight, not
deadly as grace. White mottled black,

sand in its claws, its land-lurch.
Out at sea, great ships in their lanes,
bristling with lights. I doubt those
on deck looking in at the shores

would see this monument, the writing
on the walls. They might say 'Batavia Coast'.
They might think of mutiny and death.
They might think of eyelight

shining out at them, a trick of sea
and spray and sun, glinting of sand
especially brought in for the occasion,
making new history to write out again.

Three Poems on Armour

KNIGHT'S ARMOUR AT THE FITZWILLIAM MUSEUM, CAMBRIDGE

From sabaton to visor, greave to rerebrace:
> (*He knows but one direction!*)
His family call him cyborg, but lack imagination;
He's all metal until an enemy punctures

His undercoating. Chain mail is satisfying
> (*It breathes . . . is coldly sweaty,*)
It imprints on skin or aketon a cartography
Of craftsmanship: he goes to his maker

Well unmade, having driven an economy.
> (*Museums maintain downpayments.*)
In an idle moment he marvels over rivets:
The movement of the poleyns: vital as his kneecaps.

As mirrors of his joinery, steel plate makes faith:
> (*God's handiwork given a good workover.*)
Detailed, custom-lined, in *his* own image — moreover,
Performance enhancing, product placement:

Chivalry! He's the complete package.
> (*He's thrown down the gauntlet.*)
He removes his cuisses and faulds,
And enamours us with his tenderness:

[321]

Cheerleaders, weekend warriors
        (*Paintballers outside office hours,*)
Paragliders, scrappers, war gamers,
Dealers fighting turf wars. Soldiers.

        (*Impact of mace on plate shatters peace.*)

The hundred-year flood-level would test
its grip — pinioned to concrete in a green field,
space of rest and play. A silver canter, zest
of a foal, war-weary soul sealed
in metal, hollow eyes fixed, annealed
like suns in retreat, charging past children
swinging high out of sandpit — above raised
riverbanks and pine trees — on through the town,
fighting arthritic welds, futurist prison

of cogs locked into place, springs
that won't stretch, never retract. It hears
no birds, though white swans and crows ring
its bells. The wire-mesh stomach hungers
for grass, filled instead with leftover wrappers,
drink-cans, dead condoms. It doesn't know
this place, is confused by the atmosphere —
the stilled, algal river . . . dull bisque glow
of harvested hills, roads bloody with heat haloes.

Its speech consists of silent letters,
mouth always open, ears cocked . . . some try, walking
the park alone, bending down, lending an ear . . .
some want the ear to bend their way, stroking
the bright mane and whispering

to someone lost, elusive — best-kept secrets. Time
stretches for singer and listener . . . lamenting
and praying, wanting revenge . . . the grime
of their breath congeals, forms a dull amalgam.

Here, they make horses work.
No exception. Stallions are gelded. Mares
run into the dirt. The aged sent to lurk
in paddocks beside vats and towers
that stink so bad drivers and passengers
wind up their windows when rushing past.
Iron horses — stuff of memorials — never cower
when faced with fireworks, a blast
of spray-paint, comparisons to glories lost.

The hundred-year flood-level would test
its grip — pinioned to concrete in a green field,
space of rest and play. A silver canter, zest
of a foal, war-weary soul sealed
in metal, hollow eyes fixed, annealed
like suns in retreat, accepts its place
of rest — trapped — moving forward —
shadows burn its reflective surface,
whisperers of communal grace.

DÜRER'S RHINOCEROS

Rhinoceros of childhood seen through thick bars
with sandpit and wagtails, zoo savannah or grasslands,
country compacted to a round peg in a square hole,
resigned in flesh if not eyes — vacuums of desire,
armour the leathern shields of the most ancient myth,
army writ into the single body that carries all
before it. And this Indian specimen, courtier
of language and war, limbs of what *we* imagine
as Sanskrit, resilient exotica, impenetrable with fear.
Second-hand, Dürer made this beast his own
for centuries, never witnessing its drowning
in wild seas, shipped from pillar to post, its second
skin armour on armour, body sculpted, riveted
with bones and cartilage, scales and ivory,
immutable overkill, moulded for comfort
and flexibility, sheer engineering that makes
a gift from king to king, general to general, give
and take of manufacture and manoeuvrability,
statement of homegrown technology you'll think
twice about before taking on. Even dismantling
and back-engineering you'll pull up short — it bears
no imitations. The weight of creature and armour
drive the horn deep into any Achilles' heel, affirmation
of vengeful gods: metal breastplates and cuisses,
backplates and faulds without chivalry you recognise,

like that unfamiliar vestigial horn — clitoral,
to be stroked in violence? — forced to perform
for the royal crowd, artist's impression. You saw
those eyes as a child, behind thick bars, with sandpit
and wagtails, a zooscape shouting 'there are only
a couple of thousand Indian rhinos left, whereas
in Dürer's time there were at least half a million'.
Cause and effect. It would be over sixty years after
the 1515 capturing in ink before another such
sailed to Europe. No longer the prototype,
despite the novelty. Dürer's truth: guardian of spices,
myth incarnate, embodiment of wars Europe was
preparing for. Anatomically suspect.

Two Poems for Peter Porter

VIXERUNT

come out of Vincenzo Foppa's *The Young Cicero Reading* (c. 1464)

And yet, to have lived so much already,
the gentle weariness of an angel
who has seen lengthy warring
between good and evil,

but can't wrinkle, can't take
the rouge from his cheeks, though
reading over his experience,
tightens eyes and concentrates

to be free of his condition,
and yet relish it. Optimism
is the default position, like sowing
the wheat crop into dust

and hoping rains will come,
against predictions. You make
your own luck, and luck so made
is logic. Living is knowing.

And now, young Cicero, creating
your precedents, halo of foliage,
poise stark as any window,
tunic soft against architecture,

the case is outlined: who
threatens the state, the heart
of the republic, will be
silent. The good of the people

is the good of the state,
is the state of well being.
The evidence stacks up.
Pragmatically, in the end,

you'll ask for the cut to be clean
and swift. Here, in the provinces,
we are easily distracted by the promise
of outdoor living — what quality

of air, what perfumes — your hair
helmeted, still as anticipation.
We listen for birds: now thornbills,
now butcherbirds;

but nothing distracts you,
young Cicero, from your reading:
serene as a room, the sky
dark and light at once,

this bower, this cave, where
criminals are disposed of quicker
than words, the silence
of your learning;

so, master of Rome in waiting
who is not of Roman origin,
whose words will heal and kill,
who cannot shelter beyond

senatus consultum ultimum.

The Ambassadors

In cold weather we are as large
as our clothes make us, warding
off failure with diplomatic immunity,
exploring limits of the plenipotent.

We describe for our hosts the place
we come from: its large and many
weathers threaten its coastlines. Inland
is an entirety inside an entirety,

ad infinitum. An island, yet it is endless.
Yes, there is a great heat that underlies
all extremes. Yes, we retain red dust
under our fingernails years after

arriving in the Great City. Our
tastes are not lavish — we will acquire
books and tickets to the theatre,
and sack galleries for their spiritual

worth, but keep social standing
out of discussions. We *will* visit Saint Paul's
and wonder over Donne's sermons,
but no hint of Apostolic Nuncios

[330]

will haunt our office. We will offer
up raw materials, generations
of the well-fed. We will admire
the Old Country's astrologers

gazing up through smog,
bringing heaven uncomfortably
close to earth. Back home, our
skies are *so* wide and *so* shining . . .

we remind our hosts at moments
of triumph — 'Water Music'
on the Royal Barge, the Sex Pistols'
performance of 'God Save the Queen' —

our skies are *so* wide and *so* shining.
The embassy ends before it's begun
and yet is never complete — the skull
we bring with us shines through canvas,

our skin, and as we ascend the stairway
to hand in our resignation, the skull
comes into focus — *so* wide, *so* shining,
so willing to trade across harrowed oceans.

Wattle

Every year the bright
tremor of wattle,
yellow light
yellow rattle

of stamens and pollen,
collective memory
blocking-in
understory.

This profusion
of a short-lived galaxy
provokes effusion
and heresy:

choking drought,
whirl of gases,
clearer's rout,
godless

astronomers;
neither good nor bad
can come of it: it lures
us into sacred

utterances: confess
the yellow light
is not bright
enough, or stress

the yellow light
is too bright,
far too bright
for our limited sight.

Caveat

There's a caveat on the living trees,
but don't chop up the dead wood:
especially not the trunks stretched
hollow, homes of snakes and echidnas.
When it rains hard they drum a bold
message, and when the wind stirs
through these sacred woodlands
they pipe like great church organs.
That's *your* patois.
Understand. Understand.

Maralinga

Hell is hollow, a gesture in a flat surface lipped in, the curve upturned — no same point if you keep going in the same direction; convex lore coated longer than words and longer than belief. A weeping tree in flower, a minuscule tree among the saltbush and deceased. A camel skeleton hunched big-boned against the track. Spirit-killer? It's a weapon they'd test a few times at least. Watson siding as water only here was apertured into lexical theft, before and after, to make the big bang, negate and relegate the gathering tribes — a plan — atomic warfare against a people so old they brought fear to investors in peerage, shock wave propelling the train slightly faster once out of Watson, where the first flock of birds seen since yesterday overfly warning markers, pink and grey galahs their chests shields worn in the x-ray rooms, all nature is conflated in the atom and there's no half-life of logic to ward off the insecurities. Clear sky thunder. The name retains. A given name. A Christian name. Exposure to the energy source of God by any sectarian configuration. Mirage of treed islands run blue, like a leak from the sky, blue blood shining over the expanse. Seriously, that's what you see: a spreading blue across the Axminster texture of the plain, as they would envisage it. Still holding the data, using it not an end in itself, down the track. That line of hills to the north. What do they hold back on the edge of the plain, the hollow bones.

De-fencing the Block

We're pulling the fences out
from inside the block and opening
the fenced zone to the kangaroos
on the reserve — they favour the sand
of the old horse arena, making hollows
to stretch out in under the peripheral shade.
The kangaroos follow the same patterns
even after the fences are removed — jamming
their bodies between granite boulders
and where the fenceline was, not yet risking
a spreading-out, a taking-hold of what is theirs.

Stephen and John convinced me to buy a pair
of Maun fencing pliers — almost a hundred bucks
but they'll cut through high tensile strands
with ease. Through galvanised Cyclone Wire.
Ringlock fence, star pickets at fairly
narrow spread because this is a hillside
and it's hard to keep the tension. Every
so often a join in the fence grippled together,
a logical place to stop and start again
but we move on past, wire-ties unravelled
from star pickets, and the mesh rolled
into cylinders of light and polygons.

It's bloody work — my hands are a mess.
It makes me sick of reading poems about fences.
Or thinking poems about fences. As I cut away
with the Maun pliers — the hardest steel from England —
I mutter under my breath and John asks
if I am composing a poem. He's got used
to my patterns over the years. I often ask
him technical questions about tools and practicalities . . .
Probably, probably, I mantra, unhappy with myself.
He has invented a device for rolling the top wire
and that's his poem — unthreading the strand,
whipping back through the eyelets of star pickets,
then tying off into tight coils for later use. But where?

The kangaroos are gathering. Stephen and John
pulled down the electric fencing last week — removing
wire, insulators, energiser. The fence inside the fence.
The kangaroos have worked this out; now they're
on the inside as well. Both sides at once. They are not
strange animals. Poems from Barron Field to D. H. Lawrence
have done them no justice. And which species?
Here, it's Western greys. There'll be local Nyungar
songs that make sense, speak to the kangaroos, warn
them, celebrate them. I am sure if sung as strange
it will not be a 'genuine strangeness', or a 'weird melancholy'
or a grotesque or ill-conceived hybrid creature.
I could fact-check, but this is of the moment.

[337]

I am hot and burnt and have been rolling ringlock fencing
and have just seen a large male roo and a smaller female roo
and a joey not long out of the pouch. There are no sheep
on this block now — they left weeks ago — though
bones and lumps of wool lie about. The neighbours
will ask who or what will keep the grass down?! I say,
kangaroos eat! Some shoot them for eating crops.
Work it out. A syllogism. Still, we must mind our Ps and Qs
and not insult those who would keep the roos out,
who bust a gut erecting fences you'll tear down.
But then, my script is like cut wire
flailing about — only dangerous as you
let it be, but dangerous, if briefly, nonetheless.

Goat

Goat gone feral comes in where the fence is open
comes in and makes hay and nips the tree seedlings
and climbs the granite and bleats, through its line-
through-the-bubble-of-a-spirit-level eyes it tracks
our progress and bleats again. Its Boer heritage
is scripted in its brown head, floppy basset hound ears,
and wind-tunnelled horns, curved back for swiftness.
Boer goats merged prosaically into the feral population
to increase carcass quality. To make wild meat. Purity
cult of culling made vastly more profitable. It's a narrative.
Goat has one hoof missing — just a stump where it kicks
and scratches its chin, back left leg hobbling, counter-
balanced on rocks. Clots of hair hang like extra legs
off its flanks. It is beast to those who'd make devil
out of it, conjure it as Pan in the frolicking growth
of the rural, an easer of their psyches when drink
and blood flow in their mouths. To us, it is *Goat*
who deserves to live and its 'wanton destruction'
the ranger cites as reason for shooting on sight
looks laughable as new houses go up, as dozers
push through the bush, as goats in their pens
bred for fibre and milk and meat nibble forage
down to the roots. Goat can live and we *don't know*
its whereabouts. It can live outside nationalist tropes.
Its hobble is powerful as it mounts the outcrop
and peers down the hill. Pathetic not to know
that it thinks as hard as we do, that it can loathe

and empathise. Goat tells me so. I am being literal.
It speaks to me and I am learning to hear it speak.
It knows where to find water when there's no water
to be found — it has learnt to read the land
in its own lifetime and will breed and pass its learning
on and on if it can. Goat comes down and watches
us over its shoulder, shits on the wall of the rainwater
          tank — our lifeline — and hobbles off
          to where it prays, where it makes art.

Reptile Life

A reptile book is a way of saying language
isn't tired in your hands, looking up a species.
Photo ID or running a finger down an index.
Eyes, skin, elision. What tongue twists its warning.
A book of riddles in that old between-the-epochs speech.

We measure life by their presence — snakes
and lizards. They ripple gloss across the pages,
exfoliate granite. Quiet in the biting sun.
But beneath a boulder, an easement cupping
a blue-tongue skink, the largest I've ever seen.

What do we say to that? Nothing in the pages
to correlate. Brandishing in the shade,
smoothed to cool and breathing slowly,
travesty of winter in mid-summer apostasy.
It watched with one eye and paced its heartbeat.

Without religion, we make our exegesis
out of amateur herpetology: those shiny
pages, measures of scale and thermoregulation.
Heating or cooling, we exclaim the wonder
of observation. It fits the picture and outgrows it.

Hair

'prolific hybrids have been produced'
     – Thoreau ('Brute Neighbours')

Surveying the reserve again after hearing gunfire
I come across a large thatch of hair — a headful,
quantity and weight-wise — neatly poised on the fire-
break. I look at it closely — chocolate brown, strands
wavy and of an in-between length. I look around the area,
lightly and hastily. Gunfire persists across the valley.
I've got to tell somebody though I am not sure
what I'll actually be telling them. It is so weird.
And, seriously, disembodied. The looming granite
and concerted York gums provide an atmospheric
part *Picnic at Hanging Rock*, part *Wake in Fright*.
The soil of the firebreak as it winds decisively
down the hill is deeply red but infertile. A stale
blood that nurtures only the specific, the familiar.
The thatch of chocolate brown hair doesn't sit
comfortably. I walk home and convince Tracy
that she should take a look. Absorbing the view,
semi-panorama that catches you, she crouches
and examines the hair. From one side, then another.
It seems to me to take longer than it should,
inducing a form of apprehension. 'I think it's
animal hair,' she finally says. I re-examine
and notice matting and congealing beneath.

Goat. Or an exotic 'item' of stock from a hobby
farm. Hoicked there by a fox. Eagle to line its nest.
Just statements made without conviction. *Possibilities.*
We agree that it's not human — or that it's very
unlikely to be human. And if it were, what would it mean?
Hair on a firebreak out in the bush. Gunfire continuing.

Sacred Kingfisher and Trough Filled with Water Pumped from Deep Underground

'It is the work of art nearest to life itself.'
— Thoreau ('Reading')

With the record heat I filled one of the three
concrete troughs — mainly for kangaroos
but also for birds and anything else that passes
by. This morning I saw a sacred kingfisher
in an overhanging branch, eyeing the water.
The sacred kingfisher saw me and remained.
That's unusual — they are mostly cautious.
I over-invest the 'sacred' in their name — name
giving, name evoking statistics from those
who've probably not even seen the bird. A small
bird with a large beak that could inflict a lot
of damage on whatever it targets. Proportional
and relative. Its colours are flashy and stunning.
What part do I play in filling the trough, once
for sheep and horses? How much choice
to come and go does the sacred kingfisher
have? Would it be here if the trough was empty?
The valley was quiet in the broadest sense.
I did not know how much noise was within
the bird's head. I thought of Thoreau
thinking of Alexander the Great carrying
the *Iliad* in a special casket. Which now

makes me think of a coffin. Water troughs
look like coffins, like caskets. I expected
the sacred kingfisher to swoop as if the shallow
water held nourishment. It was dead water
from deep in the earth. The sacred kingfisher
stayed in the branch, seeing the trough
for the coffin it was. The bird looked at me
then looked back to the lifeless surface
of the water. Still . . . so still.

Red Shed

'who built our red barns so admired as emblems'
                    – Hayden Carruth, 'Marshall Washer'

People hereabouts distinguish 'our' place
by the massive red shed that pronounces
a ledge hacked into the hillside: erected
by the previous 'owner', it yells cultural
anomaly across the valley: I know how
much she loved horses and dedicated
it as a stable, but I am not sure if she ever
visited America and drew inspiration
from the red barns of folklore and utility.
After years living in red-barn mid-Ohio,
we knew what red barns said to locals
and visitors alike. Here and now, they say:
sticks out like a sore thumb! Or: hey,
you know the place, the one with the dirty
great red shed! The air force use it to sight
for bombing runs. Pure terror. In truth,
it's a placid red, though the horror
of hunkering down in bush, of wanting
not to be noticed, makes it anathema.
Each day it holds sunlight between
itself and an imaginary horizon
that curves with the hills overlooking
the greater Tooday valley. Imagine

the structure of what would have grown
there if the red shed hadn't staked
a claim? The runoff from its gently
pitched roof, the red music it makes
in high winds, bleeding arteries
that feed reservoirs we drink from.
This memory of America won't depart,
and the red Colorbond steel that holds
a postcard portrait, folklore that makes work
and horses and a shelter for all weather
speaks resistance: in the worst fires
it *will* buckle and melt, but the sum
of history, its loud declaration, remain.

Kangaroos in Torchlight

Stillness makes you shiver inside, skin
unmoving; there is no part of our biographies
feeding the torchlight, only the kangaroos
trying to look gently past the flickering beam
at what's moving, what makes light out

of darkness; they don't get to select
their deaths and call it 'madness' or 'okay,
I took the risk', they just try
to stay out of its reach. In this
is the only immense spirituality

I believe, walking the long road
up the hill to close the gate, to close
in and protect what I'd like to think *they*
pass over, like our oversubscription
to the soul's persistence, or that some

memory will stick to rocks and soil,
stay close and bear light that seals
a nightworld in place, that we might absolve
the shaky clinginess of gravity: rather, all
imagined is partial indifference

of kangaroos by torchlight, stilled
to graze the dead grass of Elysian Fields
where nothing can die again, and few
will head back to that overwhelming light
that weighs so heavily on the living.

Mea Culpa: Cleaning the Gutters

Not quite believing that rain would come
in thimblefuls never mind buckets, pre-
dawn deluge, cracking of the skies
with essence of light made out of absolute
darkness, took me unawares. I'd learnt
not to believe in forecasts, to doubt
even the particular movements of birds.

Not quite believing that rain would come
I'd left cleaning the gutters, while lamenting
the emptying of the Great Tank down to its final
rung, or reaching its echo full-blown, grown
to fill an emptiness, replete with sound,
those final drops of silt and leaves that settle
having found their way through pipes to brew.

Not quite believing that rain would come
I had to wait until the last gasp of thunder,
brace the ladder, and work my way around the house,
circumnavigate and excavate the gutters: black silage
scooped and flopped to the ground — inky and indelible
even on sand. And then down to the trap to release
the filth, and scouring even the Great Tank's top itself.

Not quite believing that the rain would come
I lose time and water and watch taps flow brown.
Mea culpa, Thomas the Doubter, and whatever negative
affirmations run through my head. Cut by the tin roof,
I have only one hand free to revise what's been
hastily done: bloody hand dangling at my side,
useless and polluting as I waver near rain and sky.

Envoy

ON MELODECLAMATION

How has the stony earth
so effectively hidden the bones
of the people who came first?

Maybe the stones
are those bones
and we can't distinguish —

or won't — the sounds of native birds
accompanying our words,
fulfilling our wishes.

Tropicbirds

Here, on the island, it's the white-tailed
tropicbird, the *paille-en-queue*, with its straw
tail tillering updrafts of ravines, or pivoting
volcanic rock-faces. It resonates. But on a tiny,
flat atoll in the same ocean, I once saw red-tailed
tropicbirds, signature tails cutting sunsets,
papercuts in heavy clouds, the criss-cross
of bloodshot eyes. I am told they're here also —
nesting at the far reach of their domain —
but I doubt they'll show themselves. No flash.
No epiphanies. No past as bright as your future,
a redlining. But the white tails I see everywhere:
the slash where stone rises hot into colder air.
I lose the tone of whiteness to sunlight, and follow
its arrow west, witnessing its own will and testament,
quill to sign off and to affirm islands large
or infinitesimally small, maybe going under;
their ocean-tide's climb and descent.

Bats at Grand Fond

Tide swallows beach and even gentle breakers
push through from the reef over the lagoon
and darken the shore. The sun has left its cloud
and collapsed into a ruddy mess below the horizon.
We walk up the sandy passageway onto Avenue
Leconte de Lisle, and the pings of sonar catch
us at sharp angles, placing us in the depths
of Grand Fond, wings clicking to maintain
an illusion of invincibility; hunting mechanism.
Tim's first sighting of a bat. And there's no mistake.
The one signals many, a cloud outside meteorology —
storm warning or aftermath; a weather known to locals —
calling us out, to stand transfixed but insist that we
should move on, adjust our spiritual gain.

Ghostly as the claws of quick crabs on coral sand.
Evasive as *cabots sauteurs* on black volcanic rock.
Rectilinear as wooden pallets tossed-up on steep
beaches where no reef protects from the deeps.
Molosse bat? What *we* call 'freetailed bats'?
Likely, but there are also *Taphiens de Maurice*
and a cemetery by the sea, where prophets
and homeless men sleep by tombs, staring
out to Madagascar and Africa, over unfathomable
skies. Maybe these *are* Mauritian Tomb Bats?
We hurry home. Did you see any white
on their chests? I ask. I don't think so, Tim says,
but it was hard to tell as the last light went fast.

Ode to Margouillats

Green stone gecko with red handprint
of whatever God might be in our minds —
still as rock made by great pressure
but delicate as all-encompassing eyes;
suddenly to animate, lurch at a rival
and drop it from the cliff wall.
The *tick tick* at night is what we will
have of him — triumphant or fallen —
resonant embodiment in REM sleep
of his perfect stillness interrupted.
Journey to the Centre of the Earth
exploited lizards in its own way,
producing dinosaurs that live
in matinées, as cult figures of a future
that won't happen. *Tick tick*, he calls.

Palm Elegy for Jim

Palms thrive in the *Garden of Eden*.
They are pure escapism but loyal
To their roots. It is a dry zone
In the wettest landfall on earth.
On the east of the island it might
Be torrential while in this west, thirsty.
Some have gone troppo here but this
Would be your sobriety. A liberation,
Planting palms in the Perth suburbs,
Lungs filled with chemical dust,
Pay-packet sitting open on the table,
Two televisions tuned to rival
Stations going at once, watched
From beneath. Exhaustion is complex.
Plotting your journeys, lush palms
Wavering on screens we don't see.
Palms thrive in the *Garden of Eden*.

Bellier & '28s'

for J-F. Samlong

The bellier's imperfect yellow is survival —
the swooping flash of the sleek but pendular
'28' is as much; the dye in feathers makes words
and imagination draws flight, which you wished to do,

and caught on the ground, glued the exquisite
village weaver to the spot, not to return
to its suspended house, its next generations.
And auditory ossification. And to strike

with stone — or a stick! I comprehend
this unholy act, this false deliverance. It's our
traumatic synchronism. I can read
this much of me in you. To lift.

It's a role I imagined for myself, a Crusoe
contradiction: to shoot the birds I loved,
to wear garlands of their feathers. To bring
down from heights to flap on the dirt,

nub of grey tongue forcing apart its hooked
beak, claws grasping at twig and the small dust
clouds its dying kicks up. And to 'finish it off'
with a stick, bludgeon to be 'less cruel'. The face of it.

From that dry heat to your steamy coastline,
stone heart rising to a peak of tropical snow.
From one island to another, with all islands
they contain. It's easy to make comparisons.

But easier to declare differences. No bellier
where I come from: those wide expanses.
And now, at fifty, I cherish every bird,
every flight, every flash of colour

I can or can't identify. And if you visit
us in the wheatbelt, I will show you the beauty
of birds I once killed. I have seen your ghosts.
No atonement, just bloody images, true colours.

Sack

Ancient river bed hacked and carved whittled deep
by winter run-off river as sudden as a dust storm
in the long summer red bed red dust caves haunting
level best upper storeys where sea breeze ratchets
off ocean and estuary black bream spiky and petrifying
in their pools cut-off omphaloi each and every one
an oracle of seams and joins worked by heat rising
and stretching to breaking point the ripple and crackle
of segregation; onto the sandy riverbed soft and cool
to feet when waded through like frothy low-level surf,
encapsulated by shadows crosshatching from river
redgums in nooks and crannies down down
from ledge, onto sand the flung sack came down on,
its pulsating and cavorting arc, aerodynamic mischief,
anomaly in flight to parabola and plunge to thud
and be absorbed into white sand reddening as hessian
soaks up last breaths and catfights and mews into grey
currawong and red-tailed black cockatoo distraction
and camouflage, seed-eaters and carnivores mixed
to a pitch of blur. And witnessed by teenagers mucking
about after school: sack wrenched straight from car
lurching on dirt track a lover's leap moth-eaten or chewed
to disappointment, the sack hurled up and down down
with such force the face of perpetrator lost or encrypted,
the type and colour of car forgotten, number plate
unthought of; just the sack now twitching between pools
shallowing with heat and red motes and litotes in the air,

choking and irritating, down down onto the cool sand
(sandals kicked off), to cut open the stitched-up sack
with a pocket knife and reveal the mince of kittens
all trauma and extinction and two or three
with mouths carelessly wired together, half-open
half-closed so their noises would come out all wrong.

Blue Asbestos on my Bedhead

We always knew someone who knew someone
who could get me what I wanted for my rock collection
and pride of place was given to the large chunks
of blue asbestos a certain someone retrieved
from the Wittenoom tailings heaps. Icons,
they sat on my bedhead for years, propping up
my bedtime reading — exquisite seams of crocidolite
sandwiched between iron oxide bands. Plush, soft waves
of fibres I prised apart and rolled between my fingers:
I smelt it and tasted it and cherished the irritations
fibres made in my skin. In my wardrobe lurked
an imported piece of white asbestos I'd swapped
with another kid. So, some rocks are worth
worshipping and others not? Art overflows
with representations of death's beauty.
I built cubbies from asbestos sheeting, smashed
it up to enjoy the brittle vulnerability of the solid.
It's a long list of industrial and domestic encounters.
But the violence I must look back on in my leisure
moments is the blue confusion of glow and absorption,
the soft-hard confusion of my childhood: fibres
so small they can break into a chromosome,
speak to the most complex and basic level
of who we are. It's the tweak of a collector's
conscience, the breath I exhale on us all,
the odd cold of the iron that would have
cracked my skull open had it fallen

on to my sleeping head, the swirl of imps
and sprites and angels less blue in the crystal
haze, freed from their amianthus bundles.

The Fable of the Great Sow

Great Sow, who squashed dead her litter
A year before, rubbed her thick sparsely haired
Hide pinker than pink against sty walls.
Flies and pig smells wrought hot under
Tin roof, wagtails working their way
Between pigs and dust and shit, picking off.
To cut across her pen was an act of dexterity.
A leap across the gate, a pivot on the wall
Opposite, and over into a neighbouring pen.
Short cut. I could have gone around. But
I'd done it before, and she looked so distractedly
Blissed in her deep scratch that I took the plunge.
Many times my weight, and half my
Stretch again in length. Reacted quick
And cut me off. Back then it would have
Been easy to talk of her malevolent eyes,
Her snotty nose, her deadly teeth.
Of all human warp embodied.
My wits were dulled. She was total pig,
Pure sow who'd farrowed litter on litter
To watch them raised to slaughter.
Fed on meal and offal, she'd been penned
With boars merciless in their concupiscence.
She had a reputation for violence against humans:
She loathed them. Us. Thirty years later,
I see James Ward's painting, *Pigs*, in the Fitzwilliam.
That shocks me into recollection. Grossed out,

Exhausted Sow, eye to the light made night
With a forward ear, milk-drained, piglets
Piled sleeping by her side, eternally confident,
Her Self replete in their growing natures.
Even the runt snuggles content in straw
As there'll be plenty in her sow abundance.
She has manufactured. And as Great Sow
Is about to charge and crush and tear
My childhood out of me, I take this picture
From my future, a painting from 1793,
A painting from nine thousand miles away,
Maybe in a place where Great Sow's ancestors
Planned their vengeance, passive for the artist,
Brewing generations of contempt inside.
A point of singularity is reached, epiphany
In straw and swill-filled air between us
(Normally, I would gate her out to change straw
And water). We both grunted and she went
Back to her scratching. I scurried out, neither
Runt nor star of her litter, her old fury lost
To pig history, flies and heat of the shed.

Morgellons

Jorge Luis Borges translated Thomas Browne
into seventeenth-century Spanish. I read this
in an interview with Daniel Bourne, whom I know
but haven't seen (in Ohio) for many years.
Borges told Daniel, that 'I' — then 'we' — 'took
a chapter out of *Urne Buriall*' and rendered
it unto, or maybe in the manner of, Quevedo.

The slippage was in the Latin, as is the slippage
in the hairy children of '*Languedock*, called the *Morgellons*',
noted in Browne's 'Letter to a Friend', and sourced
to name a hairs-under-the-skin scourge of modernity,
seen by some as 'delusional parasitosis'.

The spread of this disease is concomitant (we read)
with that of the web, a metaphor for invasiveness,
to catch by proxy or suggestion. The psychosomatics
of living in the windfall of uranium decantation ponds
at Narbonne (*Colonia Narbo Martius*), commune
of Languedoc-Roussillon, where we would have gone

with its '*Languedock*'-like spelling, our nine-year-old
prey to uranium hairs that grow unseen, undeclared,
only just recognised. Precise or imprecise as a word,
a coinage of a learned and inquisitive stylist
of the English language; Romantic irritant.

Sleeping with a Southern Carpet Python

Driving south to stay with my brother in the house
on the edge of great Dryandra Forest, refuge
of the stripy termite-eating numbat, I grind the gravel
across the one-lane bridge with its brief bitumen
respite, working strobe-lit shadows and corrugations,
keeping the vehicle centred. I am a young, embittered
father moving away from family ensconced in a low
and swampy suburb, a reclaimed rubbish tip at the base
of the Scarp. Now, eucalypts and parrots cluster
at the roadside, sheep working gnomic lines to dams,
the tinge of green of the new growing year, rancour
of salt scalds — I convince myself all call me home.
I grow steadily distracted with the brute subtleties
of dragging the back end of the car into shape,
a soft spot in the gravel pulling away from direction,
gyroscopic interlude. And then, before me *within*
braking distance, within the realm of breaking thought
to control the slide without three-sixtying into oblivion,
is an eight-foot Southern Carpet Python at full stretch,
slowly negotiating the road, its cryptic rippling
a camouflage separated from its realm but working
black and gentle yellow-olive into the orange of gravel,
willing the gap to close, openness a trauma to be filed
under 'instinctual', an inverse constriction of mind
over matter. I skid right over it, crushing its tubular
body. I handle snakes. I have handled snakes since
the time I was warned not to go near, not to *touch*.
Deadly dugites and mulga snakes by the tail

[365]

or behind the head. To carry to safety, lift from roads
where they are . . . crushed. And this great snake,
distressed and writhing, python in need of a meal,
winter shutdown fast approaching, I lift and place
in folds of a tartan blanket on the back seat. Compacted,
splayed, its body hasn't burst: its hunger a blessing.
I drive to my brother's, where I place it deep down
within my sleeping bag. Warmth. (I still drank back then.
Heavily. And to oblivion.) When sleep drags me
to my sleeping bag, I don't think twice about crawling
in with the crippled, dying python. My life is lived
with sleep in glimpses, moments of nodding off,
so any sleep that comes is sleep I embrace — a sleep
with snakes is not a temptation, nor a loss. Insomniac,
I sleep deeply and in a dreamless stupor, though it has
since fed my nights with images and dark rumours.
Living dead, I still make body-warmth and the cold
blood of the snake exchanges its knowledge,
its stock of stories and experiences. When I wake
with the morning streaming coldlight into the room,
I shudder with poikilothermic thirst, clutching
the walls of my cocoon close, synapses tuning
to the expectation of snake at my feet, retracting
my toes and huddling to a ball. Emptiness.
I reach for my glasses and focus. The Southern
Carpet Python, carpet snake of my childhood
I saw often on the farm coiled around log rafters
in the hay barn, rat-hunter and friend of the farmer,
warder-off of ill charms of presence, is sliding
alongside the walls, rounding the square room,
full of my body-warmth and raring to go.

Penillion of Riding Past the Radio Astronomy Observatory Amidst Hedges and Fields

Rabbits bolt back
Into the sack
Of shade, the grey
Penumbra may

Be a shelter
From space litter
Or some deep truth
Offering proof.

The sun is low
And hedge leaves blow
Red on the road.
Croak of a toad

Out of kilter
With cold's trigger:
Hibernation?
Observation

Of large and small
Arrays brings all
Cataclysms
And charisms

Into the range
Of rooks with strange
Penchants for glare
And curvature:

The dish hearing
Beyond the sing-
Song of the lone
Bird through the groans

Of the great flock
Flooding the track
Of light to dark,
To silence stark

As the traffic
Vanishes, marks
Revolutions
Of wheels and suns.

The sun is low
And hedge leaves blow
Red on the road.
Croak of a toad.

Penillion for Pussy Riot

Faux fathers take
Pride away, rake
In the money
Quick fast and pray

Dead souls to make
The count, forsake
Their liberty.
'Security'

Is the serfdom
Of the kingdom
On earth: weapons-
Grade big truncheon

Penetration
To boost nation
Of God Father
To spite Mother.

Shake, rattle, roll.
Kiss sacred scroll
As if worship
Is the fillip

To topple self-
Styled god Himself,
Master icon
And his henchmen.

Penillion of Tuning the Harpsichord
(for J. Mattheson's Harpsichord Suite no. 12 in F Minor as tuned and played by Dan Tidhar at the Fitzwilliam)

Head tilts to strings
beyond setting —
cross-notes of talk,
gallery folk

don't block his ear
from its pleasure,
its pulling sound
into the round.

But it's finer
in F minor?
When the baroque
improv invokes

an arched eyebrow
as you follow
hand-key-notes-ear,
the busy choir?

Legomenon
sounds out of tune
but in syntax
attunes *hapax*.

Such temperaments!
Circle of Fifths.
Helix of Fifths.
Spiral of Fifths.

Pythagoras
conscious of bliss
sharply detects
the imperfect:

but the comma —
here on offer — ',' —
is harmony
not euphony,

cacophony,
or just any
note of grammar —
sounds make measure

as semantics
defines critics,
tuning keys for
pins so eager!

All things being
equal, we cling
to pitch our fate:
front 8 back 8

choir unity,
the purity
of his intent
with instrument

of our belief:
the ear's relief —
bridges to cross
rich without loss.

Penillion of His Last Harpsichord

Last harpsichord,
Name on the board:
The Rubio
Continuo

Outliving flesh
Notes will enmesh
And map our days'
Intricate ways.

Suite by Rameau
Virtuoso
Timbre and glow
Innovator:

Each note's heart plucked,
Each vessel rocked
Below the cliffs;
Polyphemus'

Eyeless fury
Drives the story
As Cyclopes' grief,
Engenders strife.

Scored cadenza
Hands crossover
The inner choirs
Of composers

Each of us must
Become — artist
At the keyboard
Enacting needs

Quickly rising,
Scintillating
To the surface.
Over his face

A distant night,
Musical light,
Of an eighteenth
Century synth-

esis of sound:
Listen, the sound
Of our applause
Ghosts our presence.

Loss

IMM David Ngoombujarra

The warmest death
As night's cold wreath
Spreads under pines
And ocean brine

Coats hair and skin
With temptation:
It resurrects
And genuflects

As seagulls glow
And pupils grow
Smaller, smaller,
Stars and mirrors

In the numb dream,
The inward gleam
Of performance
Within the dance,

Within desert,
The harbour streets,
Where time shifts gear,
Brings dry place near

To sea, brings you
Near to us, true
In our land-pattern,
Far less certain

Than you tempting
Fine dust stretching
Out with laughter
Fading, after

After.

Penillion of Cormorants in Polluted River

Wings out to dry

Those snake-necked birds
Perch on absurd
Protrusions, test
Pillar and post

Eyeing *below*,
Plan and follow
Their beaks deep down
Past light, then crown

Metal surface,
As shadow splits
Like mercury —
As mercury:

Wings out to dry

Ailing fish skive
Making each dive
Easier . . . then
Fruitless — those thin

Skins so rattled,
Their contents dead
Before being
Killed off: seeing

[377]

Their own dead-ends
As whose Godsend?
Bright red speedboats
Would have us gloat.

Wings out to dry

And nesting trees,
Dead colonies:
So few are left
Here, blue eggs lost.

Who feeds baited
Fishhooks to pied
Cormorants, fish
Still in distress?

They stare further
Than disaster,
Their bald raven
Revolution.

Wings out to dry

Penillion of the Iron Ore Eaters

for the Yindjibarndi People

It's an eating
And a shitting
Analogy?
A synergy

Of compulsion
And revulsion?
Feeding nation/
nation feeding.

Those billionaires
Work the figures:
Divide, conquer/
Coffins, coffers.

Red ore engorged,
Flowers blooded,
Wild contusion
Styled transfusion;

The vast 'donor'
Left hollow or
Gasping for breath:
Smelters are stealth

Out where the sky
Is primary.
The bands, the seams,
Layers of dreams:

Laws of *plosion*
Exploration,
Peg-claim: *purvey*
voyeurs' surveys

A deletion,
Or extinction
A tenement
As testament?

Miners' terror:
Stygofauna.
But not the 'law'
They can pay for.

They eat bodies.
They shit corpses.
Acacias.
Budgerigars.

Penillion Approaching Zennor Head

'At Zennor one sees infinite Atlantic, all peacock-
mingled colours, and the gorse is sunshine itself.'
                                        — D. H. Lawrence

That gorse sunshine
Engorged harsh on
Fish and kestrel,
Bristol Channel,

Dolmen, mermaid,
Stone overlord,
Those restless clouds
And moorland shrouds,

Edgy crossing
Of bridge spanning
Landslide allured
Into lost words

Reclaimed violet
Flickering lost
Granite bruised sea
Where near every

Echo reflects
And intersects
What we crosscheck
From buried wrecks,

Flotsam broken
Bells' devotion,
Rough cliffs angling
All winds' weird song;

Thin paths mirror
Pulveriser!
And old codgers,
Those tin whistlers.

Penillion of the Burra Dust Devil

At the corner
Of old Burra's
Dry St Just Street
And Market Street's

Deciduous
Trees with new leaves,
All recovered
Copper-coloured

From the dead pit,
Curved beige hills stripped
As the Monster's
Nobs & Snobs stir

Ghosts in old ground
Just the same, sound
Of dust devil's
Brief, rich reign: still,

Then manic rush:
Lust for a stoush,
Turn inside out,
Rage, brag and shout!

At the corner
Of old Burra's
Dry St Just Street
And Market Street

The dust devil
Sucks leaves until
Trees are bare, smarts
Its devil heart.

The Stephen Whitney:
Wrecked on West Calf Island (51.28N/09.31W)

'She went to atoms.'
  – Thomas Allen

Stacked with clouds and light's colour wheels
Awakening day to night's curing of wood & flesh —
nothing held together, and unwound springs
of clocks sprung from their cases and marked
no time, foodstuffs & cotton lost to a hungry sea.
    She went to atoms.

What grows nacre where bodies are taken down
from tip to tail, some washed up to be counted & buried
on an island boat just above the waterline, as a famine
ship coming back spills its cargo & people, the 'weather
thick', that full-rigged vessel of the Red Star line.
    She went to atoms.

In the realm of hunger a calm sea is a storm you
just can't see — the next day, bales of cotton float
past the 'miserable huts' where survivors sought sanctuary:
anatomy of the coast rising up but keeping close
to surface, the sundial houses of skin & bone.
    She went to atoms.

'Mouths all Coloured Green'

'No spectacle was more frequent in the ditches of towns, and
especially in wasted counties, than to see multitudes of these
poor people dead with their mouths all coloured green by eating
nettles, docks, and all things they could rend above ground.'
— Fynes Moryson in 1601

When we were broke
and living 'down South'
in the shack, we boiled
and ate nettles and dock.

Our watertank poisoned
and the greens tainted,
we grew sicker by the day.
The 'boys' wanted us out

of the district, our mouths
'coloured green'. The English
starved the Irish on the order
of the Queen, ditches full

of the green-mouthed dead,
surfeited on 'all things they
could rend'. A template for
the Great Chain of Being.

Above board, below ground.
The 'boys' and their families
defended Queen and Country,
joined the military. Grotesque

is a quality of patterns
and not an act of decoration.
Is it improper of me to suggest
correlations – my ancestors
    famine migrants?

Oileán Chléire Rejuvenation Poem for Gráinne

It's been a hot, stretched-out day at Jam Tree Gully.
Most of the harvest is in, though hay fever is still at full strength.
Ringnecked parrots and thornbills are threading light airs
with their evening rejuvenation songs — even birds
born in hot places relish the cooler evening. The light
is sharp and harsh and inflective — once in your eyes
it never leaves. So far inland from the sea, it's the light
that takes me to Oileán Chléire — that light taking
in all that's south, that reaches out, the most ancient
lighthouse, and takes it all back in when night closes over.
In the shadows of cliffs, the turquoise sea gathers
its strength, relishes landmeet. In the spray comes light.
To send this message through the string between two tin cans,
I check the weather report using this site your dad
put us on to — wind is 11 knots from the northwest,
wave height around 2.3 metres, it is cloudy and 5 degrees
and around 1mm of rain is possible if not expected.
From this information I can create something of a picture.
I can see the guillemots circle, I can imagine the thoughts
of the ferry's captain and crew as they consider the passage
to Baltimore, and I'd like to think I can work out where
seals are likely to be bottling. Maybe I am overconfident!
But there is the light, and I've never anywhere in the world
seen so many inflections of light. It's the many moods
of Roaring Water Bay, it's the calf islands, it's the Mizen,
the Celtic Sea, the Atlantic, the red sandstone statement
of Mount Gabriel. It's the island's surroundings as much

as the island itself. But it's the island that takes it all in,
then releases it like flocks of guillemots, that has watched
from its privileged point for so long. Signal tower,
holy well, ringfort. Ancient churches. Roofless
farmhouses. The stacking of stone on stone that rearranges
the fabric of the island itself. Restless multifaced sea.
Stonewall patchwork communication devices long
functioning without electricity. Pieces of a puzzle.
I read on an old photo zoomed up from the harbour,
a portrait of young Tim and the island behind him:
'An Ghaeltacht' and 'Trá Ciaráin'. There's a trace
of smoke from furze fires, the furze-bound walls
climbing away, climbing up into the blue light
of lookout, green tussocked fields folding light
into sods, deeply rutted trails showing that what
we see so clearly is more hidden than we can accept.
We know that place. But not like you, looking across
from Schull every day, thinking of the lexicon of place
forming in its schools, its rock. To think, I read an account
by an English minister who failed to understand the schooling
of presence — he was more concerned about the neat house
of an English compatriot. But I did learn one thing from
his nineteenth-century account — that lake, that mysterious
lake implanted in the island rock, is supposed to clean anything
(he said the islanders never needed soap!) — even oil will be
turned to perfume. I wouldn't suggest there's any magic,
but stories generate hope, I reckon. They tie all things together.
There are so many stories from here — the Noongah people
know how it all fits together, and the cost of pulling it apart.
Stories can speak to stories, rock to rock, and guillemot to parrot.

So here's a rejuvenation poem. It holds no special properties,
and there are no subcurrents — just marvel at the difference
between here and there, yet a shared wonder of light,
a familiarity of difference. As I listen to the birds here
after a brutally hot day, you too can look out towards
Oilcán Chléire and take in light, stone, guillemots,
the old ways and new ways, the energy of all places
focussed in where you are, where you'd like to be.

Acknowledgements

Thanks to all the publishers who have supported my work over
the years in Australia, UK and USA, and for original publication
of these poems. Thanks to WW Norton for permission to reprint
poems from collections still in print. Nothing has been selected/
extracted from my verse plays or 'long poem' books/works such
as *The Benefaction*, *Sacré-Coeur*, *Divine Comedy: Journeys Through
a Regional Geography*, *Syzygy* or *Rapacity: A Death's Jest Book*.
The poem 'The Stephen Whitney: Wrecked on West Calf Island'
is for the West Cork photographer John D'Alton. I wish to thank
Churchill College, Cambridge University, where I have been a
Fellow for many years, the University of Western Australia where
I am a Professorial Research Fellow, and also Curtin University,
where I am Professor of Literature and Sustainability. I also thank
Kenyon College for the years I spent there and all that it gave
me. And thanks to the many journals I have published with over
more than three decades. Thanks also to the many dedicatees of
earlier collections. Special thanks to family members, particularly
Wendy Kinsella, Stephen Kinsella, Tim Kinsella, John Askham, the
Wheelers, and Tracy Ryan. Also to my editors over the years,
including Wendy Jenkins, Ray Coffey, Jill Bialosky, Neil Astley,
Rod Mengham, and Don Paterson at Picador, who has helped me
see poems, and the collecting of poems, anew – thanks so much.
Special thanks to Harold Bloom for selecting and introducing my
previous selected poems (2003) – his generosity and brilliance are
always with me. And the erudite and scintillating Marjorie Perloff,
who has opened so many doors of thought for me. Thanks to
George Steiner, a wise, illuminating and provocative voice always,

and a centre of genius at Churchill College. I thank friends, colleagues, fellow poets, and critics, all brilliant, such as Tim Cribb, Michael Hulse, John Kerrigan, Philip Mead, Drew Milne, Clive Newman, J. H. Prynne, Susan Stewart, and many others. Thanks to Rosly for the tale behind 'The Coconut Story' (much respect!). I would also like to acknowledge the editorial support of the late John Forbes and the late Peter Porter. I wish to acknowledge the traditional owners and custodians of the land/s I write. I wish to acknowledge the land itself and all that it is. I wish to celebrate cultural and creative diversity, and to respect the environment.